NOZA: A True Basketball Success Story

To: Elijah

Never give up!

David Egger

NOZA:
A True Basketball Success Story

By
David Espinoza

E-BookTime, LLC
Montgomery, Alabama

NOZA: A True Basketball Success Story

Library of Congress Control Number: 2008925727

ISBN: 978-1-59824-798-5

First Edition
Published March 2008
E-BookTime, LLC
6598 Pumpkin Road
Montgomery, AL 36108
www.e-booktime.com

Contents

Contents

ACKNOWLEDGEMENTS

I would like to thank God the Almighty. With your guidance I had the energy to write this book about my son.

To my late wife, Candi R. Espinoza, thanks for the love and for helping me raise Matt for nine years and Jake for eleven years. Those were some of the best years of my life. Your wonderful memories will always be in our hearts, God bless and R. I. P.

To one of my wonderful sons, Matt Espinoza, thank you so much for allowing me to write this book on your successful basketball career and for the key information you provided to me that I missed. I hope that your story encourages a young basketball player or a parent. I love you son, your future is bright.

To my other awesome child, Jacob Espinoza, thank you for designing the cover of this book and for helping Matt develop the basketball skills throughout the years. Your basketball experiences with Matt were a lot of fun to write about. I love you son and keep following your dreams.

To my wife, Loni Espinoza, thank you for the help in editing this book and for coming to so many of Matt's basketball games with me. I am so lucky to have fallen in love twice in a lifetime. I love you sweetheart; you are the greatest P.E. teacher alive.

To Julie Erickson, thanks for helping us find a tournament team that Matt could play in when he was in sixth grade. You helped us get him into the competitive basketball tournaments.

Thank you to all of Matt's coaches during his grade school and Jr. High days especially Mark O'Neil, Bobby Bones, Bernie McCallister, Steve Erickson and Gib Gilmore. Your time coaching was appreciated very much, and my son had a great time playing for all of you.

Thank you to Coach Kevin Taylor for selecting Matt as one of the members of the McNary Freshman Basketball Team, and for giving him the opportunity to play in his first high school basketball game. Also, thank you to Bob Jones for coaching Matt his junior year on the JV basketball team, that year was a great experience.

To Coach Jim Litchfield, thank you so much for allowing me to interview you. You were such a huge part of Matt's basketball career at McNary High School. Thanks for selecting him to be part of your basketball program. It was a blast watching all of the games and watching him grow as an individual and as a basketball player.

Thank you to Coach Joel Perkins for asking Matt to sign a letter of intent to play basketball at Southwestern Oregon Community College. Matt really enjoyed playing basketball there for two years.

To Coach Brian McDermott, thank you so much for asking Matt to sign a letter of intent to play basketball at Southern Oregon University. You and your wife's support will never be forgotten. I think he really enjoyed the veggie meals you cooked.

FOREWORD

By Jim Litchfield
Head Coach, Basketball
McNary High School

I was thinking the other day about the time I first knew of Matt. He was hanging around his older brother Jake, who at the time was a freshman. Jake would come to open gyms with his buddies and there would be Matt shooting baskets and watching his older brother.

I also remember Matt coming to the McNary Kid's Basketball Camp, which was usually held early in the summer at the high school. We hold this kid's basketball camp every summer in the off season. It's a nice camp for younger kids to learn the fundamentals of basketball and also to play basketball games all week. It would have been the middle school years that Matt attended the kid's camp.

Matt's freshman year in high school I was aware of him just barely making the basketball team and at the time I was the junior varsity head coach. I was not at the freshman tryouts, but knew of Matt from the kid's camp he attended in the past. I also knew of him as Jake's little brother.

Matt's sophomore year I remember the JV (junior varsity) boys basketball tryouts. I was still the JV head coach at the time and during the JV tryouts my observation of Matt, well, to be honest, physically he was not as good as some of the players that were competing for a spot on the team. He worked hard, but was not very big, quick, or fast. He was a good kid with excellent grades in school and had a lot of heart.

What we knew about his older brother, Jake, is that he was a great athlete and he was tall. We thought Matt could possibly grow taller in the future. I remember Matt working so hard and he had a great shot, he could really hit the basket. Physically and skill-wise he was not an athlete yet and hadn't matured yet.

During the tryouts I watched all the competitors, and Matt was one of those players that could really shoot the ball well, but he was a lot slower and shorter than most of the group. We wanted to keep him around for a couple of years to see what could happen. We knew that he really loved to play and that basketball was a very big deal to him. We also knew that Matt would not get too upset if he didn't get playing time, just because of his character. We felt like he knew he could possibly get a chance to play someday, and he would get better.

The coaches were always honest with the kids here at McNary High School. One of the hardest things for a coach to do is to tell a kid he didn't make the team. Basketball players would always get an explanation of why they didn't make the team and what they needed to do to improve. We encouraged kids to come back next year and try again.

Tryouts normally lasted a week, when the tryouts were over Matt had survived the week. We sat Matt down afterwards and had a talk with him. We explained to Matt that he had great talent in the way he shot the ball, and there weren't too many kids that had that ability. We also told him that some kids never play, but the way he worked so hard and the way he treated other kids gave us a thought of what he could become in the future. We told him that was enough reason to keep him on the team, and we were so glad we did. It was nice having him around, and to this day it's a real pleasure when he comes to visit us at the school.

Matt's sophomore year I didn't do anything different with him than I did with any other player on the team. We just worked on fundamentals, shooting the basketball, making good decisions, passing the basketball and defense. Matt had really good instincts and was very easy to coach.

It was Matt's sophomore year towards the middle of the basketball season where he finally got an opportunity to play more. In most of the previous games he played very little. It was during a game against rival South Salem High that one of our starting posts sprained his ankle in the second quarter. It was a close game and Brody Hess had to leave the game with an injury. What most kids don't realize is that opportunities come up, whether someone gets hurt or fouls out of the game, etc. Matt was one of those kids that waited for his chance, he never gave up.

Between his sophomore and junior years you could see that he was starting to physically mature and get better. He was starting to make plays that he could not physically make the year before. The thing about Matt is that he never gave up, even though he took longer to mature than most players, he just kept at it and he knew that he was not going to be denied.

Matt's junior year we played him on the JV team and gave him the opportunity to play some varsity, but it was mostly JV that year. We felt he still needed to get stronger to earn more playing time at the varsity level. Larry Gahr was the varsity coach at the time. He had plans to transfer to a new school that was being constructed. He would become the new coach for West Salem High School. I would soon be the new varsity coach for McNary basketball, Matt's senior year.

In December of his junior year I sat down with him and told him that I would need a post next year. I felt that as much as he had improved and if he could improve that much more over the next year he could really contribute to next year's varsity team. I also told Matt that I wanted him to start eating healthier and to not drink soda pop. Matt fulfilled all that I asked of him between his junior and senior year. He lost about 15 pounds but it was deceiving because he replaced it with muscle by lifting weights on his own.

That summer before Matt's senior year I had him work on shooting from certain areas of the court. I would design a play for him where Josh Erickson, our point guard, would penetrate to the middle using Matt to set a screen for him. Matt would roll out to the three-point line and if Josh was double-teamed, he would pitch it out to Matt for the three-point shot. I knew that we were going to be deadly because with Matt playing post and being able to pop out at three-point range, we would stretch out defenses.

I met with all the kids that were going to be seniors. I talked to them about what they had to do to get to where we wanted to be. That group of kids really loved to play basketball. A majority of that group played a lot of basketball during the summer. That made my job a lot easier.

I coached many kids during my twenty years of coaching basketball. Out of all those kids, Matt was a unique individual with an enormous amount of desire to win. When you look at where he started and where he is now, and going on to play college basketball, it's amazing that he became a starter in college basketball. He just willed himself, he worked so hard to put himself in that position. That was the thing that I remember being different than the rest of the kids I ever coached.

He eats healthy, he works out regularly and he is a great person to be around. He never was envious of the other players on the team and attention focused on him was not important. Matt did what had to be done to win. His role on any given night could have been getting rebounds, or making good passes, playing good defense against the biggest player on the other team or scoring twenty-two points. To him scoring the most points on the team was not a big deal at all. He would rather win than score the most points. Those are the qualities that just not any kid has.

I feel that Matt will be very successful in whatever he does in life. He is a great example for younger kids to follow and learn from. He is very determined and he wants to win. You can have a kid that is 6' 8" and can jump and is quick and I would think that is pretty special. But you take a kid like Matt who was given a certain athletic ability and through hard work he got the absolute maximum out of what he was given. To me that is very special, that says a lot.

All the kids I've coached have had talent, but none have gotten what Matt did out of what he was given. He is part of the reason we were successful his senior year. Matt was a key part of the team and part of the reason we made it to the State Championships in 2003 and placed 4th out of 16 teams.

FOREWORD

By David Espinoza
Matt's Father

Matthew W. Espinoza was born in Salem, Oregon, at Salem General Hospital in 1984. He was a special addition to our family. Matt had a brother, Jacob, who was two years old, his mother Candi, and me, his father. Matt was a very healthy baby and always seemed to be full of energy and wanting to learn more about everything.

When he was four years old he read his first word, "Meat," in the meat section of a grocery store. That was due to all of the hours his mother Candi spent reading to him and his brother. She would also help them pronounce words when they read. I remember her reading Bible scriptures to the boys before bedtime. She would always ask the boys questions about the Gospel she read, in a fun way. I think Matt became a very good listener because of that.

I remember Matt playing outside. He was wearing some shorts and a baggy t-shirt that had spots of dirt all over. It was cold and rainy and he was getting wet but having plenty of fun running up and down the sidewalk. Candi yelled at him, "Matthew! Get in here right now! You're getting wet and you're going to get sick, it's cold!" Matt did as she asked, but was not happy about it. Later that night Candi once again yelled at Matt, "Matthew time to take a bath, get in the tub!" Matt responded, "Mom, I just want to do what you ask, I can't take a bath I will get wet and get sick." I thought it was funny and started chuckling.

Candi and I were high school sweethearts and we both played basketball in high school. She enjoyed the game and was always looking for me to show her how to shoot the ball better. She was also very smart in the classroom. I was very athletic and I had been told that I shot the basketball very well in my days.

Being around sports all my life I witnessed the good things that kids can learn and benefit from in the present as well as the future. Some examples are college scholarships, teamwork, social skills, good sportsmanship, work ethic and exercise. You can also learn how to accept losing a game and being a good sport about it, as well as winning a game and being a good sport. There are many more benefits; the list goes on and on.

I felt both my kids could possibly have a chance at a basketball scholarship or an academic scholarship. I could work with them and develop them for basketball as their sport. Candi could help on the education side, it could happen. I knew that it would take a lot of work and that somehow I could hopefully make it fun for them.

At this point, that was the plan I had for Matt and Jake. Candi understood and she agreed with me. She also told me that I had to allow them to try other things. I agreed with her, but only if I could build a basketball court in our backyard. I felt if they were playing baseball or soccer, or any other sport, they would still be able to shoot baskets in the backyard in a relaxing way. Our plan seemed to be working because whatever time of the year it was I would come home from work and hear such a great sound in the backyard. Matt was playing basketball with Jake and some friends.

While I went to work, Candi stayed home with both boys. She spent a lot of time teaching them how to read and how to play educational board games. I was the one that started showing Matt how to shoot and dribble a basketball. His older brother Jake was more advanced in those skills. Matt watched Jake and learned some of the basketball skills from him as well.

Matt started learning how to shoot a basketball when he was about two years old. I remember him wearing diapers and shooting a beach ball into a homemade basketball goal I built using two-by-four inch boards with a regulation size rim bolted to the boards. Candi thought I was crazy doing that, because Matt was only two years old. She just laughed, and as long as our child was having fun she was very supportive.

I picked basketball to be the sport Matt and Jake would play. I guess because of all the great experiences I had growing up with it and the excitement of being part of a team. I also enjoyed the spirit of it all. I played three sports in high school, football, basketball, and track and field. In football I played at the next level as a field goal kicker, I was being recruited to play at Oregon State University as a field goal kicker and punter. Craig Fertig was the OSU Head Coach at that time which would have been the year 1978. An injury to my ankle sidelined me for a long while. I settled going to Chemeketa Community College and majoring in Computer Science with a minor in Theatre Arts.

Later in 1985-1986, I played Semi-Pro Football for the Salem Stars and had really good stats. I had an opportunity to try out for a USFL professional football team, the Portland Breakers. I made the team, however the league did not last and folded. To me it was all very exciting, fun and rewarding.

Just hearing the fans after a made basket or running past the goal posts for a touchdown. Kicking my personal best field goal 56 yards against the Spokane Fury in Spokane, Washington, was amazing. All of this just made me feel really good, and made me feel a sense of a huge accomplishment. Although I played football I didn't encourage my kids to play. Football was a high risk for injury and I didn't want my kids to take the beating I did.

With basketball I believed my two boys could experience all those things plus have a chance for a college scholarship to get a decent education, because these days without an education they would end up working like my parents did. My parents worked labor job after labor job, field work, cafeteria work, bus driver, nursing home, cannery work and factory work. I just wanted a better life for both my boys.

I did not encourage Matt to play football, simply because when he was younger he had a weak blood platelets count. Basically what blood platelets do is help clog up the blood to help the body stop bleeding. The doctor told us that a lot of kids grow out of this problem as they get older. For Matt the doctor did not recommend football just to take precautious measures. It was very difficult telling Matt he could not play football, because he really liked football. It made it easier for him when we allowed him to pass the football around with Jake and the neighbor kids.

Basketball was a smaller risk, however, we still had to be very careful with him. Basketball was a safer sport for Matt and even though he was very young and didn't understand why he couldn't play football, we were able to keep him smiling most of the time.

Matt did play soccer in first and second grade and T-ball in the same years, but minor league baseball was out of the question. His brother played baseball and did get hit on the head once. If that would have been Matt, he could have had internal bleeding. Internal bleeding inside the head could have been death threatening for Matt. That was not a risk we were willing to take.

Matt watched me play a lot of basketball in different city leagues and tournaments. I had some friends that I would get together with from time to time. We played in some big tournaments such as Blazer 3-on-3 tournaments, and the State Games of Oregon tournaments.

He was always telling me how I needed to play better defense and basically all the things I was teaching him, he would haunt me with them. That actually helped me and that was a good thing. He would always let me know if I played a good game or if I played a terrible game. He also would lecture me on his perspective of the game. He was always learning and giving me stats after the games, and this was at a very young age.

Candi and I were really huge on education, I had a degree in Computer Science and she was planning on a degree in Early Childhood Education. She wanted to become an elementary school teacher someday. We both graduated from Gervais High School, but I would have to say that she was more of an honor student than me. She was a very bright lady with a passion for teaching kids in a fun and creative way.

We both felt like our kids could get an academic or athletic scholarship someday, so our plan was to prepare them the best we could and the best we knew how. I am sure many parents today wish that for their kids, the best for them, we weren't any different. If you think about it, most parents talk about their kids and what things they have accomplished or what they are proud of.

Being Christian people, we prayed just about every night. We prayed about many things with both Matt and Jake. Matt would have a difficult time not laughing during the prayer time because his brother would always make humorous comments. Jake would say things like, "Dear Lord, thanks for keeping me from socking Jimmy in the face at recess; he tripped me when I was driving to the basket." Matt would just start giggling and could not stop. Somehow we managed to make it through our prayers. I couldn't keep from laughing myself sometimes.

PROLOGUE

In Memory of Candi R. Espinoza
1961-1994 R.I.P

In 1986 I was helping my dad remodel his house in Gervais, Oregon. My son Matt was two years old at the time. He and his brother Jake were at their cousin's house with their mom, Candi. I received a call from her and she said, "David I am seeing double and I don't know why." For years she had complained about headaches, she would throw up and feel sick. When she went to the doctors there wasn't any real reason why they would think it was more than a migraine. But this time she was experiencing double-vision.

I drove her to the hospital emergency room and left our two boys with my brother and his wife. They performed a CAT scan procedure to take a picture of her brain. When the doctor came out he gave us the news. The result was not good. He said, "She has a growth in her brain and the pressure of this growth is pushing on the optic nerve of her left eye, that's what's causing the double vision. That growth has to be removed."

Candi was immediately admitted to the hospital that night and surgery was performed to remove the growth. The next step was to take a piece of the tumor to pathology. The lab would run tests to determine if it was malignant. We were praying it was not. I was a little shocked and did not know what to think. We had two boys, a two-year-old and a four-year-old. The neurosurgeon pulled me to the side and said, "I'm sorry Mr. Espinoza, the tests came back indicating the tumor is malignant." I took a big swallow in disbelief.

Doctor Buza stayed positive, and assured me that there were all kinds of treatments and after Candi healed from brain surgery we could get started right away. I began to drive her to the hospital for chemotherapy and radiation treatments. This would attempt to kill all of the cancer cells. There was no cure for this type of brain tumor but the surgery allowed her to live longer with a chance that there might be a cure discovered some day.

After work I would come straight home to pick up Candi and the boys. We would take her to the hospital for the same treatments again. This would happen quite often and to be honest, it was very stressful and tiring. I would also take her in to get MRI's once a month for at least two years. All of this on top of taking care of two children was a bit overwhelming, but with God's help I managed to do it all.

I certainly got an education on brain cancer and all of the equipment, treatments, hospital staff and of course dealing with learning how to take care of her while she was fighting this deadly illness. Candi went in remission for about four years. For a moment I thought she was cured. I made a statement to her, "Candi I think you beat cancer, the doctor said your MRI was clean." She said, "David you never beat this kind of cancer." After that I didn't know what to say but I just prayed that someday a possible cure would be discovered.

In 1991 Candi was experiencing seizures at least once a month. When that happened I took her in to the doctor, but all they had to say was that it was probably just a little stress to the brain. They recommended she take it easy for awhile. In 1993 she would have seizures at least once a week. I was so scared, with two boys and so many responsibilities there was a lot of pressure and I just had to have faith and take one day at a time. As the seizures became more regular they began to affect her speech. That was the moment I took Candi to the emergency room. The doctors performed an MRI to see what was causing her symptoms. The MRI result showed a reoccurrence of brain cancer, it was back.

What the surgeon told us was that a mass of tumor cells had built up again and this time affecting her speech. He would have to go in again for a second surgery to remove the tumor tissue that had rapidly grown back. This was done immediately, and Candi had once again survived the procedure. I was so scared when I saw her laying in one of the ICU rooms with her head wrapped in a turban. She was shaking for a few hours before calming down. It was a sight that was very painful for me to see and I felt helpless.

When she recovered from the second surgery the doctor told us that we had to take her to Portland so she could receive more aggressive chemotherapy. Salem's hospital did not have the chemotherapy that would do the job anymore. I took care of all the paperwork necessary for this to happen. She wanted to live so bad that she was willing to try anything to see both her boys grow up and to be with them. The doctor from the Oregon Health Science University told me that he would give her three months to live. My heart felt tortured and very down. Those were the scariest words that I had ever heard.

After that visit Candi's parents drove us back to Salem, we were in the back seat and Candi was in tears the entire drive back to Salem. All she could think about was how much she was going to miss Jake, Matt and myself. She felt really bad and looked at me, "David, take care of our two boys, this isn't fair. I don't want to die, I love my family too much."

When we got back home, she wrote two letters, one for Jake and one for Matt. She put them in two envelopes, but I didn't know that until months later. She had placed several things in a box in her closet. She had begun to prepare for the worst. I was trying so hard to be more positive. I would tell her things like, "Candi there could be a cure discovered, it could happen for you." Our prayers were immediately altered for requests to improve her health.

She had a choice to either continue with the more aggressive Intravenous Arterial Chemotherapy, which is like a one day surgery every month, or to not go through that at all. She chose to go through the treatment. She wanted to try anything possible to live longer in hopes that a cure would be discovered. She enjoyed life too much not to try the treatment that was available.

She would experiment with new medical drugs to help her survive the treatments. The two new experimental drugs that she tried were, Neupogen, which helped reproduce white blood cells and Epogen, which helped reproduce red blood cells. They were both successful and helped Candi recover from the surgeries. It is soothing to know that she helped society experimenting with something that would benefit many cancer patients for the years to come.

Candi lost a long hard fought battle to brain cancer. The good Lord took her on January 19, 1994. Jake was eleven years old and Matt was nine years old. Bless her heart she never smoked, she never drank alcohol, she ate very healthy, she exercised regularly and she was a very strong Christian lady. I have accepted the fact that God had plans for her and took her at a very young age. She was only 32 years old.

I instantly became a single dad and raised both boys the best I knew how. When Matt lost his mom it motivated him to become as successful as he could be in life and in playing the game of basketball. His mom loved to watch both her boys. She would cheer for them and encourage them during the early years of Boys and Girls Club basketball games.

ONE

FIRST GRADE 1991-1992

HOLIDAY BASKETBALL
TOURNAMENT

Matt attended first grade at Scott Elementary School in Salem, Oregon. His teachers always had positive things to say about him. As parents we enjoyed the conferences and attended them just to hear all the nice things about Matt. He was a bright kid and always seemed to be at the top of his class. School conferences in Salem were held all day long so parents could go during the day as well as the evening. I remember Mrs. Webb, one of Matt's first grade teachers. She would say, "What can I say about Matt, if I had all Matts in my class it would be so much fun to come to work everyday."

During the school year I could see the disappointment in Matt's face, simply because he was not old enough to play on the Boys and Girls Club basketball league. His older brother Jake was playing in the league on a team that I helped coach. Matt was always at the practices watching and shooting on the side baskets. He would always want to help out when some of the players on the team didn't show up for practice.

Matt was shorter than most of the players but his knowledge of the game and his shooting was better than most of them. Jake was always nice to his little brother making an effort to pass him the ball during scrimmages. Matt was a lot happier knowing that Jake's coach, Jeff Hilfiker, would always ask him to help out during practice.

That year during Christmas break there was a third grade Holiday Tournament. It was a two-on-two tournament that was to be played on a nine-foot basket. When I read the flyer on it, well, I don't know what most parents would have done, but I basically told my kids, I didn't ask them I told them, "Jake! Matt! There's a tournament in two weeks I'm entering both of you in it." Matt was so excited about the whole thing his eyes just lit up! He looked at me and said, "Yes!"

He was finally going to play in some games with referees and everything! For the next few weeks we would work on some plays that he and his brother could run together, and of course we did conditioning drills, those were not fun for either of them. This was a third grade tournament and Matt was a lot younger than the other kids. To Matt it meant a lot for an opportunity to play in a real game. Never did I ever expect for this to be one of my most memorable moments with my two boys and my wife.

They ended up playing four games total, the first three games they pretty much crushed the opponents. The final game of the tournament for the championship was a barn burner. The other team had a kid that was taller than Jake, and Jake was pretty tall for his age. Matt was very short and much younger.

This game was very exciting! The Espinoza team was ahead most of the time. The rules were you had to win by 2 points with the game being played to 11 points, 1 point per basket and 3-point baskets counted for 2 points. Jake had scored most of the points throughout the game until the other team started double-teaming him.

The Espinoza team and the other team were tied 11 to 11, the other team went up by 1 then the Espinoza team tied it up with a basket by Matt! Jake was double-teamed so he passed the ball to Matt who was wide-open on the baseline. Matt caught the ball and put the shot up, nothing but net! Now the Espinoza team was up by one and needed one more point to win.

The opposing team had the ball this time, the big kid took a shot and missed, Jake got the rebound and dribbled to the left side, and again they double-teamed Jake, so once again Matt was left open, this time from the top corner of the key about an 18-footer. Jake passed the ball to him once again! Matt let it go with a nice follow through and nailed it again! To clench the championship! I ran out to the floor and picked up Matt above my head and spinned him around in the air! We were so excited! The brothers played like a team. It was an amazing experience for our family.

After that tournament I had a feeling that Matt would do some great things in the future. The rest of his first grade year, Matt had a lot of confidence and knew he could play basketball and have fun with it. He would read biographies of NBA and college basketball players. He learned so much as a young boy, even when visiting my relatives he would always be involved in the mom and dad's conversations. He would always quiz me on information he learned, sometimes I had the answer and sometimes I didn't.

Collecting basketball cards was a hobby Matt and his brother loved. They would trade cards with each other and with friends from the neighborhood. Matt kept up with the market value of basketball cards. It was a lot of fun for them and it seemed to entertain them.

We would take the boys to some of the Chemeketa Community College basketball games and some of the Portland Trailblazer's games. It was a highlight and a fun family trip for all of us. One summer we all got to meet Reggie Miller, we showed up really early and walked around to the back side of the coliseum.

We saw a taxi cab pulling up; the cab seemed to be dropping off a 6'7" NBA player. Matt yelled out to me, "Dad! There's Reggie Miller!" Portland was playing the Indiana Pacers that day and I guess we were at the right place at the right time. We got a chance to talk to him for a bit, and Candi took a picture of us with Reggie Miller.

TWO

SECOND GRADE 1992-1993

PUSHING MY SON TOO HARD

Matt would enter the second grade in good shape. The summer before second grade our whole family would often go jogging together. In addition to this we had a hoop in the backyard and shooting practice was always fun and relaxing.

I attended a coach's clinic through the Boys and Girls Club, this was the only way parents could coach a second and third grade league team. It was a one day clinic and I learned a lot about being a coach for young kids. My intentions were to take care of Matt and give him the experience of playing some solid team basketball. I would always be around him and could help him with the fundamentals. It was a fun year and Matt developed more skills in this league. He played point guard; he and another kid were the best ball handlers on the team at that age.

Most kids that age were just beginning to learn how to walk and dribble. With me coaching our team it was possible to run two plays, more than that would be near impossible for kids in second grade. If any of you have coached second and third graders, you would know what I am talking about. Doing this would give Matt an organized view of basketball and how it should fundamentally be played.

It was a tiring season keeping up with my job, working with the boys on basketball skills and taking Candi for chemo and radiation treatments. She was very supportive of all the things I was doing with Matt and Jake. Through all of the treatments, Candi was still involved in volunteering for the school, to be around our kids and know what was going on at all times. I guess you could say that we were very protective of our children.

Matt would earn top scores on all of his subjects at school and he was also becoming a very good artist. He enjoyed drawing pictures; somehow he acquired a natural talent. Most of the pictures he drew were of basketball players. Matt's uncles, Loop Espinoza and Gilbert Espinoza were artists. They drew some amazing pictures mostly of horses and western scenery. His grandmother Gabriela was also artistic, and his aunt Kelly Ward was also an artist with a creative imagination for crafts and colors. I think maybe that's where he gets it, a little bit from each family member.

While drawing pictures gave Matt a nice break from basketball workouts, I think he knew that I required him to fulfill the practice necessary to get better in all areas of his game. I felt strong about getting him started at a very young age. As he grew older he would have more of an advantage over another kid. At least that's what my plan was for him.

I had separate workouts for Matt and Jake. The workouts were separate from the team's workouts whether it was in a gym, our backyard, or in a park. I usually started them out with warming up drills like lay-ups. Then we did some free-throws to cool down a little. I had them run to a certain point and back, as they would run back I would pass them the basketball as if they were in a real game, they would then shoot the ball. They took turns and we went for

10 repetitions each, then we would shoot free-throws again to rest a bit and to emulate a game situation of shooting a free-throw in a game when tired.

I would have them dribble with the left hand and shoot, and then with the right hand and shoot. I would play defense explaining to them which way to go if I tried to steal the ball or how to keep the ball away from me. Defense one-on-one verses team defense are two different concepts, but I worked on the one-on-one defense concept with them a lot. These are just a few of the things I did with them to help them improve. It was easy for me because they were both such smart kids and very coordinated.

During Matt's second grade year, I would videotape his basketball games and his brother's games as well. One thing I worked on was to not scream at them during the games, especially if they made mistakes. I knew that coaches did not like parents coaching from the bleachers, it wasn't a good idea. So I recorded the games with a video camera instead. When we returned home after the games, I would talk to both boys and share things they needed to work on.

It was nice that I could show them what they needed to improve on, at the same time I would always praise them on all the good things they did, a nice pass or a smart shot, or even a good defensive move. To this day I am so glad I videotaped their games, because now I can still go back and watch some of their games when they were so young. I especially enjoy watching the first tournament they played in when Matt was in first grade and Jake was in third grade. That was one of the classic moments in our family history.

I have always been very competitive and wanted them to be better than good. A couple of times I lost my temper and yelled at them. I didn't feel that they were giving 100 percent. So I would make them do more drills until they got it right. I learned later that this was not the way to develop them.

One day I was reading Matt's school journal that the teacher assigned her students throughout the year. I read something that would change me and how I would work with my two boys. Matt's journal went something like this, "I like playing basketball with my family, it's a lot of fun, but I don't like it when my dad yells at me when I make a mistake." I knew exactly what my son was talking about. I was really hurt and just thinking about his mom being ill and all, made me feel worse. Tears started coming out of my eyes for a few minutes as I would start thinking about how to change my careless behavior.

I never realized that I was starting to take the fun away from him in basketball. I did change my ways and started easing up a bit on yelling if he made a mistake. Basketball started being fun again for Matt. I sure learned an important lesson from my second grade son. I truly recommend parents to listen to their children, and read about the things they write in school, especially if they do a journal for a project. It could pay off like it did for us.

We often participated in other activities at home, just to take a break from basketball now and then. I would help them on school projects and participate in school activities with them. We would watch movies or Michael Jordan NBA videos, play board games, play video games and other games. I remember helping Jake with a rap he wrote for his vice-president speech, we recorded it and everything. Matt would always help and be involved.

Music was another passion Matt and his brother had. I don't remember there being a day that I didn't hear music in the house. I would say hip-hop/rap, alternative rock, and some Christian was most of the music I heard. They knew most of the lyrics to many of the songs. I would say Jake was the rapper and Matt was more alternative rock with some rap.

THREE

THIRD GRADE 1993-1994

ALWAYS A PLACE TO PRACTICE

I would have to say that basketball was a huge part of Matt's life growing up. My experiences with basketball were different than most people. I played it growing up, but never had a lot of support from my parents, other than rides to practices and back, when they remembered to pick me up after practice. Most of the time I would end up walking a few miles home. They would rarely come to my games. When they did come to my games it was like a big light shining on my face.

Bless my parent's hearts, Wenceslado and Gabriela. They had six kids to take care of so I can imagine it was tough doing it all. I have a lot of memories of my childhood and I guess with Matt and Jake I would never miss a game unless they were both playing at the same time.

I did experience those kinds of conflicts. My solution was to alternate turns between games. A parent attending their child's event, no matter what sport, is so important, especially at a young age. It just means so much to a child.

My advice to all parents is to attend your child's games and get involved in his or her activities.

Matt was in the third grade and we had moved to a nicer neighborhood in Salem, Oregon. We moved from the Scott School Elementary district to the Hayesville Elementary district. Both schools were in the northeast Salem area, however, the new district had a house that was available for us and we felt the price was a great deal. The buyers previous to us had a loan that failed.

That year was very stressful as Candi's brain cancer had reoccurred after a four- year remission, and basically, I found myself taking care of her and doing everything else. Her mom, Elaine, and her sister Kelly, helped when they could, but most of the weight fell on my shoulders. That didn't stop me from working with my boys and continuing developing their skills in basketball.

Because we moved, we didn't have a hoop built in the backyard yet. I would talk to principals to see if we could get into the gym during the winter. We also relied on school playgrounds and parks. Somehow we managed to get to a hoop to work on some drills.

The only thing I wished I could have had more time for was helping them with their academics. Candi would be the one to do most of that, I helped a little. She could no longer do that, but I think she worked with them long enough that they developed good study habits. I think they understood that education was very important. They continued to do well in school, both boys had outstanding grades.

Matt entered all kinds of competitions, Elks Hoop Shoot Free Throw Contest, Spelling Bees, Hot Shot Shooting competitions, 3-Point Shot competitions, etc. Sometimes he would win and other times he would lose, but he always seemed to be one of the top finishers.

I think Matt would get frustrated at times because Jake would always win. In the Elks Hoop Shoot Jake advanced all the way to the Regional Championships and took second place, the trophy was almost as big as him. The furthest Matt would get was the District Championships, taking second place. The competitions would help Matt in the future and would be very rewarding.

Matt always had a group of friends he played with at school, and he would invite them to his birthday parties. During the birthday party he played games with his friends and participated in all kinds of activities. He got along with anyone and definitely showed leadership skills.

It wasn't surprising that most of the time he would play basketball with Jake's friends, because I always wanted my two boys to stay together when they played with friends. He would get frustrated at times because he was always one of the shortest ones in the group. It would be very difficult for him to get rebounds or shoot over taller defenses.

When he played his brother one-on-one, he would often get upset after losing a game. Jake was just too tall and more advanced in the game. I felt bad for Matt, but I knew it would help him in the future. To play against a better player like Jake would benefit him in the long run. I always told Matt to not worry about losing to his brother, because his brother was two years older and about eight inches taller. I felt that was easier said than done.

Matt never gave up. He always played hard and was always trying to keep up with his brother. The only time Matt would win was when Jake played lazy defense and Matt scored from long range. It was fun teaching Matt how to play defense against Jake and it was fun observing his progress.

When they played against the neighbor kids, the Espinoza boys would usually win. My kids tell me now, years later, that I used to deny them the right to play with this one kid that used to come over, because he wasn't athletic. I don't remember that, but it is probably true. All I can think is that I just wanted them to improve on their skills and by playing kids that weren't that athletic, might not help them. I don't think that's how I should have viewed things, especially with them being so young. If I were to do this all over again I would allow my kids to play with whomever they want, and not base it on how athletic they are.

During the early years we often went to the Chemeketa Community College gym. We were able to sneak in to shoot baskets and work on dribbling skills. Matt was always enthusiastic about shooting baskets in a college gym. He could do that for hours. On Wednesdays and Saturdays we often watched games at Chemeketa CC. I often wondered where my kids would play in the years to come. I thought to myself, "It would be so cool if they played here someday." I knew that wherever they chose to play, I would be there watching.

When we could not get into the gym, we would work on dribbling with the right hand and left hand on the outside part of the gym. The facility had this wide indoor hallway all around it with a gray carpet. Both Matt and Jake would work hard, sometimes I would bribe them. If they worked hard and completed all the drills I showed them, I would buy them a pack of NBA cards. I did that every now and then, but not all the time because of budget constraints.

Candi would encourage Matt to work hard and to be patient, and explained to him that his time would come. She also told Matt that he was always trying to keep up with his older brother and that she knew that he would get frustrated because everyone was always taller than him.

I remember her saying, "Matt you have to be patient, one day you will grow and compete evenly with your brother, just keep working hard, stay positive and never give up. I love you very much." She was such a great mom to both boys, they were both our priority, very important to us.

She had this caring voice that when she spoke it made Matt feel better most of the time.

Matt was brought up going to church regularly and as a Christian. We said prayers just about every night, but as Candi's health got worse it was difficult to focus. Sometimes we missed praying together, but still managed to pray on our own, we just did the best we could. Matt's mom fought a long hard battle against brain cancer. The good Lord decided it was her time. Candi died January 19, 1994. Matt was 9 years old and only in the third grade.

There would be a rough road ahead for Matt, Jake, and myself. I knew that God took her and she would be in a better place hopefully watching over her kids from above, if that were true it would be so amazing.

With both Matt and Jake playing in basketball leagues I managed to keep them going to practices. I would also be coaching Matt's team the next year, I think this helped us not to get too down; we were able to continue life.

We had our moments from time to time that we broke down, but that got better as the years passed. I speak for myself, but truly do not know what the boys were feeling. I just tried my best to encourage them and to continue the plan that their mom and I had for them, a college scholarship someday through academics or athletics.

During the summer Matt and his brother participated in Jr. Olympics Track and Field meets, they excelled in two field events, the shot put and discus. They both were state champs, regional champs and after that advanced to the National Jr. Olympics Track and Field Championships in Gainesville, Florida.

I had this crazy notion of giving them protein shakes, I think the only thing that happened is they gained a lot of weight. It might have helped a little but only to place 11th and 10th at nationals. The good part of this was that we got to go to Disney World! Never had we experienced anything like that. I couldn't believe how many foreign people we saw there.

After that summer it was tough for them to get back into basketball shape, but somehow they did it. We would go jogging around the neighborhood regularly until I felt they were back in basketball shape. I didn't just have them jog, I jogged with them. It was like setting a good example for them, plus it helped me stay in shape as well. The jog became a fun family exercise activity we all participated in.

FOUR

FOURTH GRADE 1994-1995

I COACHED TO HELP HIM DEVELOP

Matt was going through a transition of transferring to a new school, which had just been built. Previously he attended Hayesville Elementary. Yoshikai Elementary would be a year-round school. This would be the first time the school district would experience year-round. The boundaries had changed and some students would go to Hayesville and some to Yoshikai. Matt's brother, Jake, was also about to transition, this would make it very difficult for me as a single parent now. Somehow I managed to get them to school and back home, not an easy task. My job allowed me to have flexible hours which made it very nice.

Once again I had built another backyard basketball court for our second home. To save money I did most of the work myself in this major project. First I excavated the ground, which is heavy labor. I didn't mind since it gave me a great workout. I bought several two-by-four inch boards, laid them down as the baseline for the court and leveled them to a precise measurement. Once I had them leveled I braced them with some twenty cent braces. I followed that by adding stakes for support all around the frame so when the concrete was poured it would hold strong. Next I sprinkled gravel inside the frame for drainage under the concrete. Now it was time for me to call a professional concrete finisher. Since I did not own the tools to do a nice finish job, this was the most efficient way for me to complete a nice basketball court. The finisher took care of ordering the concrete and everything else. He knew how many yards to order based on the volume of the area. The basketball goal would be the last thing that I would put up. Piece of cake huh? I was able to save myself about two thousand dollars the way I did it.

We also joined a basketball facility that had just opened in town. In Oregon it rains so much that you can't always play outside. This was the best thing that could have happened to us at the time. No more organizing open gyms just so my kids could practice their skills. No more sneaking into Chemeketa Community College Gym and pleading with the coach just so we could use half of the gym to shoot baskets while the college team practiced on the other half.

This was like basketball heaven to us! The new basketball facility had six full length basketball courts to play basketball games and practice anytime of the day. This place was called The Hoop. I guess in a way that was our second home, a great place for me to also play and watch the boys.

This season I was coaching Matt's basketball team in the Boys and Girls Club League, my assistant coach Dean Morrow was a good friend, he had kids that were also involved in sports and he was very supportive of my coaching style. This was a fun year for Matt; he played the point guard position along with Nick Morrow. Nick was the other point guard since Matt and Nick were the best ball handlers on the team.

One of my goals in every game was to set up plays for every player on the team. I wanted every player on the team to at least score one basket. If it was a close game then I wouldn't be as adamant about it. I remember one game, we were up by 20 points or so, I won't mention this child's name to protect his privacy, but the whole team was rooting for him to score. I swear we set up about 10 plays for him before he actually scored a lay-up, and when he did the team went crazy! As a result, we all saw the joy in his face as he shined with a big smile. I remember his parents coming up to me after the game and they said, "We just want to say thank you so much for doing what you did with our son, that really made his day." I really feel that coaches should do things like that for kids that aren't as fortunate as others just to make them feel important too.

Matt gained a lot of experience during that season, and it helped keep his mind occupied, it helped with grieving and not thinking too much about his mom, who had just passed away.

I saw the improvement on Matt's defense, his positioning between his man and the basket was looking good. On offense, he wasn't real quick but moved well with the basketball, including seeing the floor while he dribbled. The hard work he put in all summer and all fall was beginning to payoff. Great year for Matt, at ten years old he appeared to have some skills that were starting to be noticed.

Matt was having so much fun playing in the Boys and Girls Club league. He was a little heavier than the year before. I would take him and his brother to fast food places more than usual, I guess it was quick and easy. We still managed to eat healthy from time to time. I wish I could go back in time, the diet would be much different.

The eating habits would change later when Matt was more educated about healthier foods. I'm hoping that my son will forgive me for feeding him fast foods and allowing him to drink too much soda. I did keep up the fruit, vegetables, and milk. I pushed milk a lot as it made the bones strong and helped him grow. Anyway, sorry I got off on the diet thing.

After the games we would go over the great things he did in the game as well as the mistakes he made. I felt bad because I just wanted the best for him. I knew he had talent and sometimes I felt like I was pushing him too hard. Sometimes I would get upset and raise my voice at him. He was starting to show signs of not having too much fun.

I started noticing that he knew exactly what I was going to say after every game. I would say, "Matt, if you're wide open, shoot the ball! You are an excellent shooter." Sometimes Matt would respond with tears saying, "Dad I already know, you don't need to keep telling me." Or sometimes I would say, "Matt if a kid is quicker than you are, sag back a little and cut him off, force him to shoot from the outside." He would respond, "Dad I know already, I don't want to talk about it."

I felt like I was too hard on Matt and at times I didn't think about how he might be feeling after losing his mom; it was still fresh in his mind. Also because his older brother was taller and more dominating at his age, I would forget that Matt was only a fourth grader and very young.

Like everything else I learned quickly what caused my kids to get upset. Later that day, like a lot of times, I would find myself apologizing to Matt for being so hard on him and moments later we were laughing and joking around again. Listening to my child was very important to me.

We had a great father-son relationship and I think he knew that I loved him very much. I would always tell Matt that the reason I yelled at him was because I knew he had the ability to do better and in the future it would help him in high school basketball. I knew how hard it was to play varsity basketball and how competitive it was. I guess that's why I worked so hard in preparing Matt and his brother for the future.

Matt was too young to understand all the things that I knew, just from being around the game for so long and keeping up on today's competition from the biggest schools around. All I could tell my son was, "Matt, right now it's hard for you to understand why we practice so much and why I am always pushing you a little, but someday you will hopefully see it all."

Probably the hardest thing for Matt was not hearing his mom cheer for him from the stands during games. Candi would always yell positive things like, "Go Matthew! Good job! Play defense!" When he didn't hear his mom from the sidelines, I am sure he missed it. I learned to explain mistakes he made in a nicer way. I never forced Matt to play basketball, but I hoped that he enjoyed it enough to continue.

Not only did he enjoy basketball, he lived and breathed basketball, he had a love for the game. It was an easy job for me as a parent to work with Matt. He loved the game as a child and every year he just kept getting better. Matt would practice shooting baskets on his own and to the point that I would have to call him inside for dinner.

I started reading more of the school material from his school work and items teachers would send home. Things started to get better and adjustments were being made slowly. I was starting to pick up where Candi left off in the education world for both boys. I developed a deep respect for all stay-at-home moms that take care of their kids and do the entire housework. In my opinion, that is a much tougher job than going to work in a profession outside of the home.

During his fourth grade days, Matt would read biographies on NBA players. Bobby Hurley, who played for the Sacramento Kings, was one of his favorite players at the time. He even got to meet Bobby after one of the Blazer games in Portland, Oregon. That was definitely a highlight for him. I think we still have an autographed Bobby Hurley shoe.

FIVE

FIFTH GRADE 1995-1996

OBSTACLES WON'T BRING US DOWN

Things were adjusting a little better and Matt had started school at Yoshikai Elementary. This school was literally new; the construction of the building had just been completed. His brother Jake was also starting at a brand new middle school, Adam Stephens Middle School. That year I coached Jake's seventh grade basketball team and Matt would play his final year in the Boys and Girls Club league. This season Matt was the leading scorer for his team and was selected to play on an all-star team that the Boys and Girls Club had formed.

During the tournament Matt did not play much, he wasn't one of the quicker or taller players on that team. That's just part of life in sports and at one time or another, a majority of kids will go through that. Matt came down with the flu for the second game of the all-star tournament and did not play. It was nice that the coaches selected Matt to the all-star team, this was a great accomplishment. I am sure he would have loved to play more in the tournament, but things just didn't workout for him in that tournament.

This period in time was really a time to monitor Matt on his bruising. He had not grown out of the blood platelet medical condition. After every game he would have new bruises on his knees and thighs from getting bumped. Nosebleeds during the summers were common for Matt and sometimes he would get weak, and need rest. The cooler weather was much better, not as many nosebleeds. During basketball camps, it would always be the same story; the heat would cause his nose to bleed. Eventually this uncomfortable situation for him would stop.

Matt attended a few basketball camps through the summer. Not only did he learn about basketball, but he also learned about techniques on how to stop nosebleeds. He also seemed to make new friends at each camp. I would usually sign up Jake with him at the same camp. I think I felt better about it, especially on the overnight camps. The nosebleeds were something Matt would have to deal with, at least until he grew out of this condition. Coaches and other people he met would always tell him what would stop the bleeding.

"Don't sit back."

"Sit up and put pressure on your nose."

"Stuff a tissue in it for awhile."

Although people were helpful, it boils down to the dryness of the blood vessels inside and the blood platelet medical problem he had not grown out of yet. His blood platelet count was not enough to clog the blood up as fast as most kids. Cooler weather was much better for Matt, more moisture helped. Ice and pressure to the nose would be effective. Living in Oregon was good for Matt since it rains so much, and it is not always real hot in the summers.

When there was no school during the summer, being a single parent became tough. I found myself looking for a babysitter. My two boys weren't old enough to stay home by themselves yet. We had gotten to know a neighbor family that had five girls and three of them were teenagers. I hired the two oldest teenage girls to baby-sit my kids. Ruth and Elizabeth took turns different days.

What I had in mind is for my kids to be watched after and fed, and also to make sure they shot their free-throws in the backyard. The two girls were very nice and seemed to be doing a great job. It was still difficult for me to go to work because no matter what, I would worry about Matt and Jake. I had never left my kids with anyone other than relatives before. They were old enough now to do many things on their own, but I still felt comfortable having someone older and responsible there in case of an emergency. The two girls were also the older sisters of the kids that Matt and Jake played with from time to time.

After work I came home and Elizabeth or Ruth, whoever was the babysitter that day, would return to their home. I felt that they did an awesome job and that they helped me when I needed it. As Matt and Jake grew older I no longer needed the babysitting service. Matt was responsible for his age and Jake helped take care of Matt when I was at work. I was a phone call away and I had trained them on what to do in case of an emergency. Luckily nothing serious happened.

Probably the worst thing that happened was a water pipe broke and water started gushing in the living room floor. Jake called me at work and I instructed him to ask the neighbor to shut off the water valve, which was located on the street sidewalk. He did exactly what I asked him to do.

I think Matt and Jake became very independent at a very young age. They did things that most other kids that age did not do. They often had to fix their own meals when I wasn't home from work yet. It was usually something that they had to microwave or a cold sandwich. Cereal in the mornings was almost automatic unless it was the weekend, then I cooked eggs and toast. I wasn't much of a cook and just stuck to simple things.

SIX

SIXTH GRADE 1996-1997

KEIZER TOURNAMENT TEAMS

I had been looking around for competitive teams in the Salem/Keizer area that traveled to play other organized teams for Matt and Jake's age group. At our church, there was a parent that had a kid who was a very talented point guard. This player, Brian Zielinski, was one of the reasons this tournament team was so successful. Brian's dad remembered how well Jake had played against their team the previous year. He mentioned to me after Church one day, "You should bring Jake to our Keizer eighth grade tournament team tryouts we sure could use a player like him on our team."

Keizer, Oregon, is right next to Salem, Oregon, and McNary High School is the school this tournament team would feed into. McNary was known to have a good basketball program and was one of the biggest schools in the Salem/Keizer area. I would have to apply for an in-district transfer for Matt to attend Whiteaker Middle School in Keizer, and we would have to move to the McNary district.

I began looking for a bigger home with a bigger backyard; this would be our final move. Once I found the lot that was perfect for us, I worked with the builder to build our home. We sold the home that we had lived in for about two years. The only problem was finding a place to stay while the new house was being built.

My brother Richard lived in Gervais, Oregon, a small town fifteen miles north of Salem. His kids attended a private school there. Matt and Jake were very close to their cousins, they spent a lot of time together over the years. We somehow managed to work out a deal with my brother and his family. I would pay him rent and he would provide us with one room to stay in until our house was built. It was actually kind of fun, but crowded.

I enrolled Matt and Jake at Sacred Heart, a private school where they would learn more about God and at the same time receive a great education. This would be only until our house was built and then we would have our own home. I was stressed out to the max for many reasons, but somehow I was still able to relax and not worry so much. It's always a scary process to sell your home and buy another. For us it was a major change.

During this time Jake made the Keizer eighth grade tournament team, and I was determined to get Matt into a team. All of the organized leagues were already in progress and we didn't make the deadline on tryouts for Matt. I had to really work hard to find a basketball team for my son. I made phone calls to all of the organizers and could not find a spot for him. It was very important that I find a team for him to play on. I could see the disappointment in his face; he really wanted to play on a team. I didn't give up, there had to be an opening somewhere.

I kept calling people and asking, "Is there a spot for one more?" All I would get was, "We're all full, sorry" or "You're too late, sorry." I finally decided to call the coordinator for the Keizer A Team, Julie Erickson. She told me, "Tryouts were last week and I don't think there are anymore spots left." She said she remembered Matt from the Elks Hoop Shoot Contest, her son Josh had competed against Matt at district the previous year. She continued saying, "It would be a shame if he couldn't get on a team. Let me check around some more and get back to you." I gave her our phone number and thanked her.

Two days later I received a call from the coordinator. She said she had talked to the B Team coach. One of his players had dropped out for some reason. If they added another player the team roster would go to eleven players. It's always nice to have an extra player in case someone doesn't show up for practice or an injury occurs. But this still wasn't enough, the coach told the coordinator to ask us to come down to the next practice. He would have to go through a tryout to make the team. Only if Matt could help the team he could be on it, which made sense to me.

I was hoping they would give Matt a chance. He was in good shape and could shoot the lights out of the ball. Matt was very excited, I explained to him that he needed to play smart and showcase all his skills, defense, passing, shooting and following instructions.

I was excited because both Matt and Jake would be playing basketball with organized tournament teams that included a lot of parent's support and encouragement. Keizer was known for its community support through the years.

We showed up at practice on Monday and met the coaches. These coaches were parents of players on that team. I just watched and saw how they worked with the kids. Mark O'Neal was the head coach and Bobby Bones was the assistant coach. Matt did exactly what I asked him to do, during the warm up drills and during the scrimmage.

Once the scrimmaging started, the coaches were talking about Matt, but I couldn't hear what they were saying. Mark walked over to where I was watching from the side, and asked, "Did Matt try out for the A Team?" I responded, "No, we missed the A Team tryouts, but we would really love for him to play on this team if possible." Mark continued, "He has a nice shot and can pass the ball very well, we're lucky to have him. If he would have tried out for the A Team he might have made it." Then I asked him, "Does this mean he is on the team?" Mark responded, "Yes, welcome to our team."

It was such a nice welcome to one of the Keizer tournament teams, the teams that people would always talk about in the area, very organized and competitive. Matt went on to play with this team in tournaments all over the state. Matt had a great season with this team and gained a lot of experience.

A memorable moment came in a tournament held in Canby, Oregon. Matt's team was playing Tualatin, Oregon. Tualatin was ahead by eight points as the end of the half was approaching. Matt hit some big baskets to bring us within three points. The score was 27 to 30 with four seconds left until halftime. Matt shot from just in front of the half court line swoosh! Right after he drilled it through the net the gym lights went out! The gym was pitch-black. This exciting shot tied the game. Unfortunately it took the maintenance worker awhile to bring the lights back. Our momentum slowed down a bit and we ended up losing the game to an A Team from Tualatin. After the game I remember some people saying, "Matt shot the lights out of the gym!"

Another big tournament Matt played in was the Great 48 in Beaverton, Oregon. His team ended up placing fourth in the B Team bracket. Matt was selected to the All-Tournament Team. I was so proud of him he played really well in all the games. It was the type of tournament where they announce the All-Tournament Team at the end of the tournament.

The gym was packed and to watch him walk out and receive his trophy was a very nice memory, this was a moment that I am sure his mom would have loved to see if she was still around, hopefully she did from above. I am sure she would have been proud of her son. Those moments continued with me throughout the years with both Matt and Jake and to this day.

SEVEN

SEVENTH GRADE 1997-1998

MATT GETS PASSED UP

This would be a challenging year for Matt, and I believe that his faith, dedication, understanding, hard work and support from his family got him through this year. We were in the process of adjusting to the brand new home we had just moved in to. This would be the final move for my two boys and McNary High School would be the basketball program we would become a part of. Jake was already there and Matt would soon follow.

Matt had attended McNary basketball camps in the summers along with his brother. I would go in and check on them and ask the coaches how they were doing. It seemed like a very nice program and I knew that if my kids were thinking of playing college ball some day, I had to get them involved in a basketball program like this one. McNary was a big school with an attendance of close to 1700 students and the basketball team played in the Valley League Conference. This conference at the time was one of the toughest conferences around.

The summer before Matt entered the seventh grade, I built our third and final basketball court in our backyard. It was a nice big backyard with plenty of room for at least two-on-two games. Jake and Matt would play a lot of one-on-one in our backyard. The frustration would continue with Matt taking a lot of the beating from his older brother. Matt was too short for Jake at the time. Matt would get angry and push Jake and then go in the house in tears.

Matt would get his shot blocked and kept trying angrily to score on Jake. Matt would say, "Arrrg! Quit fouling me Jacob!" Jake would respond with a chuckle, "I'm not fouling you Matt." I tried to explain to Matt that it was good practice for him to play against Jake and to understand that Jake was taller.

Jake was always nice to his little brother about the situation and encouraged him to not give up. He would always apologize after he won the game; he knew that it was difficult for Matt not to win every now and then. The amazing thing is that once they came in the house and Matt had a little time to work it out, he was fine.

I guess my idea as a parent was to raise them as basketball players. I thought that if they did well and had talent they would love the game and continue to play. With Jake I never had to ask him to practice or work on things, until he got to high school. During high school Jake lost a little motivation for the game, simply because of losing his mom at such a young age. He thought about her a lot and struggled a bit. To be honest, it was a real challenge keeping him going. He had so much talent and could do amazing things on the basketball court, his no look passes were my favorite to watch.

They were both becoming basketball players and they were both developing their own personalities. I always wondered how they both got along so well through the years, but was very glad they did, it's a true blessing. Matt was very quiet but always thinking and observing, he always enjoyed telling me about funny or interesting things that happened at school or practices.

Jake was very social with friends but very quiet elsewhere and a thinker as well, and always had humor lines. Jake would be the one I always had to get after, especially for cleaning his room. Matt was the one that listened to me and cleaned his room when I asked. I am sure many of you parents and kids can relate to that.

I learned over time to appreciate the differences in their personalities. I would love my two boys forever, no matter what.

Matt was getting ready for tryouts, which were held at Whiteaker Middle School. There were about 150 kids that were trying out for three teams, an A Team, a B Team and a C Team. When we walked in the gym I saw some of the kids from last year and was blown away at how much they had grown. Some kids had grown three to four inches over the summer, and others had become more aggressive and quicker. I was hoping Matt would make one of the teams. Just from looking at the first day of tryouts I could tell that Matt would at least be on the B Team with a chance that he might make it to the A Team.

The A Team had two coaches, Steve Erickson and Gib Gilmore. I asked them what they were looking for, and what it would take for a kid to be on the A Team. I remember them saying, "Well, we are looking for kids that play team ball, pass the ball well, shoot the ball well and quickness for defense." At that time Matt had 3 out of 4, the ability he lacked was quickness.

The next day we received a call from the coordinator, Julie, with news that he had made the A Team. What she told me is that they were a little concerned that he was not very quick, but because he shot the ball extremely well, and he was a great team player plus a good kid, they thought he would fit in well with this team.

We were all so excited, wow! Matt was on the A Team! This was a huge deal if you were from the Salem/Keizer area. This team had a reputation of winning big tournaments and Matt would be a part of it. The team would be playing in the Salem Skyball League and the rules were, every kid got to play evenly for three quarters. In the fourth quarter the coaches could play whoever they wanted.

The Salem Skyball League games were fun to watch, and very organized. The tournament team games had no rules as far as playing time, it was more competitive and we had the type of coaches that took winning very seriously. I totally understood that because I was always a competitive person myself. I was raising Matt and Jake in a way that winning was important. We always kept score on any game we played; it was just the Espinoza way I guess.

This season was probably one of the toughest seasons for Matt. I could never understand how he was so supportive of his team and always had a smile on his face. I on the other hand, well, it was very difficult. For the first time in Matt's early basketball career, he was coming off the bench and not playing very much at the competitive tournaments.

These tournaments were composed of the best teams in the state. There would be all-star teams that were put together entering these tournaments. The tournaments were played at Sisters, Oregon; Vancouver, Washington; Beaverton, Oregon; Salem, Oregon and Lincoln City at the Oregon Coast. Matt played a little when the games were really close and when the team had a big lead he would get more playing time.

Matt's strong point was the outside shot, mostly three-point shots. The coaches at times would put him in if they needed players that could hit the three-point shots to possibly win the game. Matt was shorter than most of the players on the A Team and a lot slower. For seventh graders we had some pretty talented players.

Josh Erickson was a kid that could do it all, ball handling, great shooter and a great defender. He would go on to be McNary High School's starting point guard in the years to come. Tyler Matheson was faster than lightening and could jump like a rabbit. Tyler would go on to play college football in the later years. Ryan Rufener was a very athletic kid, good shooter, great defender and was all over the floor. Brody Hess was one of the strong post players and played tough inside. Robbie Wood was a great shooter and defender, C.J. Farrell was a great forward and Darin Smith was a powerful post player that was big and fast. These are just a few that come to my mind that played with Matt that year.

This year was tough for Matt but he never gave up and he learned valuable lessons. Matt learned all the plays the coach taught and also learned how to play better team defense. I went to most of the practices to watch. I was impressed on how these coaches not only taught the boys basketball, but also how to respect people. That was basically my life, it revolved around Matt, Jake, practices and games. My job was flexible and I could use my vacation time as requested, thank God to that.

While Jake was a dominating force for the McNary freshman team, Matt was coming off the bench for the seventh grade A Team. I helped do the clock and score book for Jake's team and I took Matt to practices and tournament games on weekends. I had to rely on some parent friends to give Matt a ride when Jake had games the same time as Matt or vise versa, this would help resolve the conflict. How I managed to coordinate everything, I'll never know, but thank God I made it work. The good conflict would continue for years since they were both on organized basketball teams.

During the year I found myself praying a lot for the safety of my boys and also feeling very bad for them. I have a good feeling that the good Lord guided both of them through the rough times. I can never imagine what they were feeling not having a mom when all their friends had their moms at basketball tournaments, first day of school, last day of school, birthdays, school award's banquets, graduations, etc. But I would have to say that I was there for them and carried out what I thought was best for their future.

I wanted them to have fun playing basketball and someday to hopefully earn a college scholarship. Matt continued practicing and this year he would enter The Knights of Columbus Free Throw Contest. He made it past the local and district competition advancing to the state competition. We had to leave a tournament game early to compete since the scheduled times were a conflict.

At the state competition it was very intense you could hear a pin drop when each kid was shooting the free-throws. When the ball bounced you could hear an echo all around the gym. Matt did an outstanding job hitting 22 out of 25 free-throws and taking the first place trophy! That was a highlight for him and we were all very proud of him. When we returned to the tournament with the first place trophy and medal, some of his teammates and coaches were yelling, "Good Job Matt! Wow!"

As the weeks went by I continued to watch Matt come off the bench in competitive tournament games. I could see that he was being passed up by the other kids on his team. He was shorter and slower than most of the kids on the A Team. His attitude was great and he was always giving the players high fives during time outs or at the end of the quarter. When he entered the game, usually with a few minutes left, he played hard and gave a 100 percent effort. Matt had a great attitude and somehow refused to get discouraged.

There was a moment in time where I just lost my cool. I probably embarrassed my son. We were at a tournament in McMinnville, Oregon. The team we were playing was a team that had the son of a university coach. We handled the team very well and my understanding was that this team was always one of the teams to beat. We managed to play very well and actually took a 22 point lead.

With three minutes remaining in the game Matt had not played yet and finally he entered the game. I was so glad to see him on the floor after a long wait. Unfortunately, he must have done something wrong, because the coach pulled him out of the game, I could see the disappointment in Matt's face as he was walking back to the bench. This had never happened before when he entered late in a game. I think we were 20 points ahead with two minutes left.

I lost my composure and walked out of the gym into the hallway, took off my coat and slammed it against the wall with a lot of anger, bam! There were a lot of emotions that I was feeling about unfairness for my son. I didn't think anyone saw me, but with the door open behind me, there were a lot of people that saw me. I was thinking to myself, "How can he pull my son out of the game with two minutes left when he just got in and we have a 20 point lead?"

A parent came after me and told me that they were putting Matt back in the game. This person felt bad for me and understood, and helped me calm down. I was too embarrassed to go back in the gym, so I just watched from a glass window from the hallway. The caring parent continued to calm me down in an understanding way.

The next day I asked the coach about it, and I was surprised at his response. I was a little hurt and felt bad that Matt had to be in the middle of all this, not to mention that he was getting ready for the finals in a tourney free-throw contest representing his team. He was facing Grayson Boucher, who is now known as "The Professor" in the And1

Mixtape Tour. Matt didn't shoot too well because of the commotion I had caused.

I remember what the coach told me after we were done arguing. He basically said, "When he gets to high school you can try complaining to the coaches there." The coach, and myself were very competitive people in general and what he said really hurt my feelings. That incident encouraged me to make a decision for the rest of Matt's basketball career. Never again did I want to go through what I did during that tournament, especially if it involved my child.

After that weekend, I never talked to coaches about Matt's playing time. I just supported them and their basketball program. This made life a lot easier for Matt. I apologized to the coach, and I apologized to Matt for my behavior. No matter what the reasons are and no matter how unfair we might think things are, the coach is the coach and no parent should ever act the way I did that day.

The best way to handle this is to set up a meeting and talk to the coach in a civil way, which is a much more professional way to communicate. In my opinion it should never be during a game or around the player, especially if he or she is very young.

I wish I could take back that moment, but I guess that taught me a lesson that would help Matt in the future. I realized he just needed to work on more skills and improve on all areas of his game. I talked to Matt and explained to him what I would help him work on. I also told him that he would grow taller in the next few years. During one of Matt's doctor visits the doctor told us that Matt would be over 6'1", he just didn't know how much taller. So I knew it would be a matter of time.

The rest of the season I just watched Matt and supported him and his team. When he played in the games I was very proud to watch him play. His team had a great season and we were smiling again. At the end of the season, the team had a pizza party. The coach said a lot of nice things about Matt and his teammates, and as always he complimented Matt on being one of the best 3-point shooters he had seen at that age.

EIGHT

EIGHTH GRADE 1998-1999

STEPS DOWN FOR PLAYING TIME

The summer before Matt's eighth grade year we would get to work on basketball skills, I often worked with him and his brother Jake. This summer would be a summer of spending a lot of time with the cousins from my side of the family. Matt and Jake got along well with them; the cousins seemed to be more excelled in track and field but were also good at basketball.

Matt played many games in the backyard with the cousins, Richard T., Joanna, Jaclyn and Jason. Jaclyn would go on to Notre Dame on a scholarship in Track and Field to throw the discus. She set many records during high school and currently holds the second best throw in Oregon high school history for girls. Candi's side of the family was not as athletic but they did have other interests that were just as important. I guess because of that most of our time with relatives was spent with my brother's family.

Matt did a lot of running as well as shooting the basketball during the summer. I worked with him whenever he played against friends, the cousins or his brother. My focus a lot of the times was for better defense and shot selection. We even had barbeques after playing basketball. Everything seemed to revolve around basketball for us.

Matt's eighth grade year we were still settling into our dream home, a dream home for us was nothing like a Beverly Hill's home, but still very nice. I had saved up money for years for a down payment for this moment. A two-story 2400 square foot home, with some modifications I made to the plan. There was plenty of room for us three and a huge backyard where I would build our final basketball court.

I put in a nice heavy duty goal with a glass backboard and a 25'x 30' concrete slab surrounded by a green lawn. This was a screaming sight for anyone that has a love for basketball. I don't want to sound materialistic, but to practice on a goal that is solid just like the ones used in real basketball games, is a huge plus.

When I was growing up in Dimmitt, Texas, I played on a hoop attached to our house and the basketball court was basically dirt. In Texas, it didn't rain very much and the ground was hard enough to dribble a ball. I had to make an adjustment from our home hoop to the game hoop in a gym, not fun. I made sure Matt and Jake didn't have to go through that. I just felt sorry for my mom and what she went through with my brothers and I after a game in the dirt, not a pretty sight in the house.

I seriously thought about putting Matt in a weight training program for him to get stronger and quicker, but I remembered reading about how lifting weights at a young age could stunt your growth, whether that's true or not I'll never know, but I didn't want to take that chance. I made sure that Matt or Jake didn't lift weights until the later years in high school. Lucky for me I didn't even have to ask Matt when he got to high school, it's just something he took on his own to get better.

Matt became the class president of Whiteaker Middle School. He accomplished so many things in academics and athletics. He even played the part of Willy Wonka in a play, "Willy Wonka's Chocolate Factory." We were starting to get adjusted with Matt making new friends at the middle school that fed into McNary High School.

My plan was that one day he would play varsity basketball for this school. Playing varsity basketball is a dream that most grade school and middle school basketball players have. I guess I would say it's a dream for the athlete as well as for the parents.

All too often it becomes a parent's dream and if the child does not find an interest and motivation for it, then the child is not very happy and there could be a struggle between parent and child. So I guess parents, try to make it fun for your child and make sure that it's not just your dream, but the child's dream also.

The day of tryouts for the A Team, the B Team, and the C Team would come again as the basketball season would creep up on us. We were excited that Matt had improved on his skills, however, he had not grown much. We walked into the gym and saw about 100 or so kids shooting baskets and warming up.

Everyone seemed to have grown two or three inches over the summer, and Matt had not grown that much. The parent coaches and high school coaches were all there. I knew that Matt would either end up on the A Team barely making it, or the B Team.

Matt had a good tryout, but he was not as quick as some of the kids out there and not as big. I talked to Matt after the tryouts and I think we both felt that if he made the A Team we would have a positive attitude about the season and just work hard to improve and get better. I don't think that Matt would have played that much in the tournaments, but he would have played in the Skyball League games because of the rules, every player played evenly for three quarters.

Luckily Matt was picked to be on the B Team. The Keizer area had a great bunch of kids to select from, so this team was pretty solid, but just not as solid as the A Team. Matt was actually very glad he was playing on the B Team, and would have two new coaches, Bobby Bones, and Bernie McCallister. Bobby was the assistant coach when Matt first tried out in the sixth grade so he was familiar with what Matt could do. On this team, Bobby's son, Bret, played the point guard position and Bernie's son, Keith, played the post position.

Matt played one of the wings and sometimes the point guard position, and once again one of the best 3-point shooters in the league. The B Team played in just about all the tournaments the A Team did. Some tournaments were just for B teams. We had a great group of kids that loved to play basketball. Matt was one of the starters playing a lot in the tournaments and four quarters in the Skyball League.

Matt was gaining valuable experience and the best part of it all, he was having a blast. They beat a lot of B Teams this year at open tournaments. The question began to pop up with the coaches, "Can we beat the A team if we played them?" We would eventually find out as we would finally end up playing them in one of the tournaments.

When that time finally arrived, we held up pretty well in the first half, but in the second half we just weren't deep enough or tall enough and we lost the game. It was a great exciting game and the possibility of an upset did not hold up. Matt and his teammates were very good sports about it as were the players from the A Team, and the coaches were smiling after the game.

I remember the time we traveled to a tournament at the Oregon coast, in Lincoln City. There were some strong winds and the power went out at the school where the tournament was taking place. The first day the games were cancelled, the next day the games were all cut to 20 minutes long with a running clock, this would cover all the games missed on Saturday.

On the way back home we had to drive through the mountains packed with snow and I had no chains. This was the first time I had ever been up to the mountains when it was snowing. We had one of Matt's teammates with us, Tyler Braun.

Often I would help out another parent or two with their kids since they did not go to some away games, this was more fun for Matt too. There was snow coming down and the wind was blowing and our van had no chains on the tires. I asked Matt and Tyler to say a prayer that we make it home safe. It was just one of those moments where we needed the good Lord's help. It helped for sure because we made it home safe. Our van was still running with only one dent from a tree branch and a mess to clean up from Tyler throwing up. He had picked up the flu while we were there, fun times.

At the end of the season, the playoffs for all the teams would take place in Salem, Oregon, at The Hoop, a huge basketball facility. The A Team ended up taking second place in their division. The B Team, Matt's team, ended up winning their division. I remember the championship game. The A Team players, parents and coaches were all watching the game and supporting us along with a big crowd that we didn't expect.

We were playing against a South Salem middle school and Matt hit some big three-point shots to help his team win the championship game, yeah! This was a great ending to a great season. I was a very proud dad that day and I still remember how great it felt to watch Matt contribute so much towards the win.

Matt had become a more confident player, he played smart and would do what was asked of him from the coaches. I was so proud of him and I had so much fun watching him develop that year. I don't think that he would have gained that experience had he been on the A Team, he wasn't big enough or quick enough to get the playing time he needed. He just wasn't ready for that level of play yet.

Once again it was difficult for me to celebrate such a wonderful year with Matt, simply because his mom was not down here on earth with us. The years got easier and I started focusing on making it about Matt and celebrating with him and his brother on his accomplishments. I just had to move on with life and make that adjustment. Her great memories would always be in our hearts no matter what for the years to come.

At the end of the season, the coach had the end of the year party at his house. The coach talked about each player and once again complimented Matt on his ability to shoot the 3-point shot, his passing skills and his improvement. I remember Bobby's words, "Matt has unbelievable range for shooting the basketball and he will be a lot of fun to watch in high school some day." That was a nice honor, and Matt was very humble about it all.

At the end of Matt's middle school days he had accomplished more than I could ever imagine. He became the class president of the eighth grade class, the Knights of Columbus Free Throw Champ, his team became the B Team Division Champions, he received a 4.0 Grade Point Average in school, he performed at a talent show playing the guitar to the song "My Girl," he served as an alter boy for our church, and I am sure there was more. But those are the ones that come to my mind. Naturally I was very proud of my son.

NINE

FRESHMAN YEAR 1999-2000

SACRIFICES TO MAKE THE TEAM

I remember taking Matt to his first day of high school, wow, where had the years gone? My baby boy was a freshman in high school. That was a day that I drove off in tears after dropping him off. I didn't let him see me but all I could think of was how his mom would have loved to share that moment with me. As I drove away I felt bad, but at the same time I felt good about doing everything possible to take care of Matt and his brother, Jake, who was a junior at McNary High School that year.

Matt became the Freshman Class President of the school and was very involved in the youth group meetings and Bible studies that took place outside school hours. Heaven forbid we worship the Lord on school grounds. I think the laws we have made in this country are ridiculous, the country that has the words on a federal coin "IN GOD WE TRUST." Sorry to get off the subject, but sometimes I just don't understand why things work out the way they do.

Matt was only about 5' 7" as a freshman in high school and most of the kids had grown pretty tall, with some being over 6' 0". I often took Matt to football games, school dances, youth group gatherings, or friend's houses for other events, especially during football season. We also played a lot of basketball in our backyard or at the athletic club.

Matt made some new friends in addition to some of his friends he already had from the middle school days. Again, most of his friends were basketball players. They would all come over and play in our backyard. Matt did all those things while he waited for basketball season to start. He always looked forward for the season to start.

Finally football season was over. It was time for basketball tryouts in early November. McNary held tryouts for the freshman, JV (junior varsity) and varsity teams. Tryouts ran about a week and cuts were made each day. At the freshman level out of 40 kids trying out, the coaches selected about 15 players to make the freshman team and that was it. From my observations, you had to have some kind of experience, or exceptional talent, or be very tall with potential.

The freshman coach that year was Kevin Taylor, and the tryouts were very competitive. A lot of the kids from the seventh and eighth grade tournament teams were cut in the first two days. Some of these kids were Matt's friends. Most of the parents we knew were disappointed that their kids would no longer play during high school. Some took their kids to play in a hoop league or at a Parks and Recreation league. Their kids just loved to play the game and that was the alternative for not making the high school basketball team.

I made a decision to be supportive of the McNary High School's basketball program and I stuck to it. I did not watch the tryouts; I purposely stayed out of it all. This to me was best so Matt would feel more comfortable. I only went to pick him up after each day of the tryouts praying he was still on the team and of course gave rides to some of his

... needed rides. For some reason their parents couldn't pick them up, I was glad to help though.

I would always ask Matt about the tryouts and how they went. Everyday I picked him up from tryouts I would be so nervous. I wanted Matt to make the team and I wouldn't even care if he didn't play that much. I knew that he would be part of the team and could work to get better. I also knew that he could learn McNary's offense and defense techniques for the years to come.

Matt would grow more, we just didn't know when. He was known for his shooting ability, but at the same time I had in the back of my mind, "What if he got cut?" That kept me up at night and it was difficult for me to get some sleep that week. I knew how bad Matt wanted to be on this team and how hurt he would be if he didn't make the team. I think that most parents out there that have a child trying out for a high school team can relate.

I found myself praying at night to the good Lord. I had never asked God for anything like this before, basically, I would pray for his safety and his strength to do well. That night I just asked the Lord that if it was his will to give Matt strength to make it through the week past the tryouts; we would be more than joyful and grateful.

The second day of tryouts Matt was in pain. His back was hurting pretty bad, I guess I forgot to mention to the Lord that I wanted him to make it through the week without pain as well. We rested him as much as possible between tryout times, but still he complained about his back aching. It was just a bad time for him to have an injury.

I mentioned to him, "Matt, let's tell the coach that your back is hurting." Matt responded, "No! No! I don't want to make it because I have an excuse. I want to make it because of the way I play." I said, "Okay Matt, but if you make the team promise me you will tell the coach so he can sit you out for a week?" He said, "Yes Dad I promise." I felt really bad for Matt there had to be something I could do.

I decided to take Matt to the doctor and then to therapy, just to be sure he could continue tryouts. The therapist explained to me that he could continue the tryouts but he would experience some pain. She said that Matt had a little scoliosis, a curvature of the spine. He could correct it with exercise and after the tryouts he would have to sit out for awhile.

We now knew that Matt could continue the tryouts. I felt so bad for him, but managed to stay positive. I explained to him, "No matter what happens, I am very proud of you and will always be there for you." Everyday when I picked him up, we would talk about the tryouts and he would give me details about who got cut and how he felt about his tryout that day. His back continued to hurt; we continued to put ice packs on it every night.

The final day of tryouts had finally arrived. Matt explained to me that one more kid had to be cut. It was between him and a kid named Jason Rabenburg. It was a long day at work and all I could think about was the tryouts. My workday was finally over and I was on my way to the school.

When I showed up I saw him walking toward our van with a smile on his face. I knew he was on the team just by looking at his face. That moment was one of the happiest moments of his high school days as a freshman. He said, "Dad! I made it!" I just reached over and rubbed his head as he was entering on the passenger side, "Matt! Congratulations! I am so proud of you! Now we can rest your back, you are on the team!"

We really felt bad for Jason. I can't imagine how he and his parents felt as it must have been a disappointing day for them. Not to take anything away from Jason because he became a great football player at McNary. He decided to pick his sport as football in the early going.

When we got home I gave my son a big hug and we celebrated with his brother and I think one or two of his friends came along as well. While we were eating dinner I told Matt not to worry if he was one of the shortest players and not as quick as the other players. I continued explaining to him that he would have a lot of time to learn McNary's program. Matt would shake his head yes as I added, "You will grow and improve in time." The glow on his face just told everyone how he was feeling and that of course, made my day. Needless to say I got a lot of sleep that night and was more relaxed.

TEN

FRESHMAN BASKETBALL SEASON

PRACTICE HARD AND SIT THE BENCH

Matt's freshman year was a mixed emotions year for me, watching Matt and his older brother Jake at the same time. Most high school gyms around here were built pretty logical. Schools have two gyms, one upstairs and one downstairs. I really felt that they built them that way for people like me. Sometimes I could just stand on the top row and see both games. Most of the time I would watch Jake's game until the fourth quarter, then I would watch Matt's game since the junior varsity and freshman boys both played at the same time.

Matt was usually one of the last players to enter the game in the fourth quarter and for me that worked out really well since Jake played the entire game as a junior and Matt played very little as a freshman. At the time I was a single parent, and that was my life, taking care of my kids and being involved in their activities. In my opinion, it's probably the best experience a parent could ever have with their children. Not only did I enjoy watching them play sports, but I was also spending quality time with them.

I had the opportunity to watch Matt work hard at getting better. On weekends, when he wasn't learning from the coaches at school, we would shoot baskets together and work on all kinds of drills. By the end of his freshman year he had improved in several areas as a basketball player; defense, offense, shooting, plays executed by McNary High School's plans and teamwork. He was slowly starting to develop into a fine young basketball player but still had not grown very much and was not very quick.

One great memory that comes to me when Matt was a freshman is the time his team was playing against McKay High School. This is the school he would have attended had we not moved across town. Coach Kevin Taylor knew that Matt was not yet quick enough or strong enough to contribute to the freshman team when games were really close. He often gave Matt the opportunity to play when the team had a decent lead.

In one of the league games the Celtics had a 14 point lead against the McKay Royal Scotts. Matt entered late in the fourth quarter with about 3:00 minutes to play in the game. He was left wide-open several times and he connected on 4 of 4 three-pointers.

I remember Mrs. Stromme, a parent from the other team. She walked up to me and said, "Does your son ever miss? My goodness he is a great shooter!" I was proud and felt a positive vibe of what he could become in the future here at McNary High School. But the patient game for us continued. I have to say that it was worth the wait. Who could have predicted anything ahead, except himself and what he had to prove as a result of his hard work and determination.

Matt wanted to start doing weights, but I refused to let him because of my knowledge on growth of the bones.

Before a young man begins weights I truly believe that the body should be at a point where it has slowed down on growth. With Matt I knew he had inches to go before he would slow down on his growth. So he listened to what I was saying and just lifted light weights and exercised conditioning drills, at least for his freshman year.

I could see the frustration my son was going through, he wanted to get better and he wanted to contribute more to the team. He was glad to be on the freshman team and honored, but at the same time I could tell he wanted to play more and have more of a significant roll. All I could do is encourage him not to give up and to keep working hard to improve.

His daily routine started to be a trip to the athletic club, where we were members at the time. Playing basketball with whoever was there, and if no one was there, he would shoot baskets for hours. I started working out and playing with him and his friends. That is what our routine started to be pretty much everyday. I often played pick up games or three-on-three games with them. If they needed an extra person to even out the teams, Matt would ask me to fill in.

At home I would play one-on-one with Matt or Jake, let me tell you, they started beating me pretty easy. It was fun playing basketball with my kids, I really enjoyed that. Today I still play with them, but not too often. I feel the pain the next morning a little more than I used to in my younger days.

I enjoyed watching Matt play, but I also gave him advice on passing the ball, how to play better defense and when to shoot the ball and when not to. But I didn't do that all the time just when I felt it was okay. Matt had a group of friends from his team that also played basketball at the athletic club to improve their skills. Trust me, he didn't like his dad giving him advice in front of his friends.

We would always get something to eat afterward, either at a sandwich place or a burger place. It was very rare that we cooked at home, because I just wasn't a cook. Some days I did manage to cook simple thinks like spaghetti, soup, or frozen foods from the store. This is basically how it would be with the three of us Jake, Matt, and I.

ELEVEN

SOPHOMORE AND JUNIOR YEARS

TOUGH WALKING INTO THIS TRYOUT

Matt entered his second year at McNary High School and basketball season had once again arrived. Tryouts for the JV boy's basketball team were set to start in early November. Jim Litchfield was the head coach for the JV team and once again there was an outstanding group of athletes trying out. The competition was very stiff and Matt would have to really do well to even have a slight chance of making the team. He had grown a few inches since last fall but still not very tall. Matt stood at about 5'10" and was a little quicker than the previous years. He had lost a little bit of weight and physically was not as strong as some of the other kids that were trying out.

The junior varsity team is made up of sophomores and juniors. I can't imagine what Matt might have been thinking walking into the gym and seeing all of the players he was competing against for a spot on the team. I knew that Matt had two things going for him. The coaches knew he could shoot the ball very well and that Jake had been very successful at McNary. Jake's height was almost 6'5" and Matt could possibly grow more to be as tall as Jake.

With all that knowledge it was still a very stressful situation. Matt didn't play much his freshman year and he was usually one of the last players to enter the game in the fourth quarter. Most of the freshman players from the previous year were trying out and some of the JV players were returning for another season on the JV team. There were also some new transfers that were trying out for a spot.

Matt would find himself in a very challenging situation. I was worried that he could possibly be cut from the JV team. I thought to myself, "If Matt doesn't make the team I will continue to help him and he can try again the following year." I wanted to prepare myself for the worst and I guess this time I tried not to think about it so much like I had his freshman year. I had a job that required a lot of thinking and I had to focus on positive things. It is a nightmare for a parent to wait for the results of a basketball tryout.

Over the years I had invested thousands of dollars towards basketball shoes, basketball camps, tournament trips, backyard basketball hoop, etc. I would lose out if my child didn't make the team. It's not just the money that was invested, but also the disappointment of seeing my child miss out on what he wanted the most, to play on a high school basketball team. I didn't want to see my child disappointed, but if he got cut from the JV team that would be part of life. That would be an adjustment that would be very difficult to make, at least for us it would be.

The interesting thing is that Matt seemed to be very positive about the tryouts each day. I started not worrying so much when I observed his attitude. Every day during the tryout week he always seemed confident. He would tell me about the drills they worked on and how he felt he was doing. He would say, "Dad, I think I have a chance to make the team, but there are a lot of good players this year. I won't know for a few days. Today some of my friends got cut, it was sad."

The last day of tryouts was finally here and Matt had survived the week, but still didn't know if he was on the team or not. After the final tryout session the coaches pulled Matt over to the office. They had a talk with him and informed him that he would not be playing much at all. They wanted to keep him around another year to see if he would grow or to see how much more he could improve. They knew of his brother Jake and that he was a great athlete and tall. They also knew how hard of a worker Matt was and by his character they made an assumption that he would get better.

Wow! He made the team again! Matt felt great about making the McNary basketball team once again. Basketball was a very big deal to him. The fact that he wouldn't be playing much didn't appear to be a disappointment to him. This time he would be part of the McNary JV team. When he told me the news I was so happy for him and all my worries would end about this adventure. When we got home, Jake and I were so excited about Matt making the JV team that we took him out to eat at a nice restaurant to celebrate the great news.

When the season got going it felt much nicer than the last season, because there would no longer be a conflict. No more watching my two boys play basketball at the same time during the league games. The JV boys played before the Varsity boys. I would arrive early to all the games to be sure I had the opportunity to watch the warm-ups and I didn't leave until the varsity game was completely over. The games made it a long night but there was no place I'd rather be than at a McNary Celtic's basketball game.

As the season progressed Matt would play sparingly coming off the bench. What he really enjoyed is the practices, because that gave him the scrimmage time, and drills that he needed to continue improving. His shooting was not an issue since he had that practice regularly at home or at the athletic club.

Most of the kids on the team were players he had played with for years. Kids like Grayson, Robbie, Josh, Ryan, Jared, Brody and Keith. That was a good thing for the future years. Teams that keep the players together develop better by the time they get to be seniors. During practices, Matt would play against the best players on the team, and he would improve on the skills he needed.

Towards the middle of the season Matt would finally get an opportunity. He had waited patiently for this moment. He had improved on all areas of his game and he had grown another inch standing at 5' 11". He was pretty close to my height of 6' 0".

We were playing rival South Salem High School and Brody Hess, one of our starting posts, came down on someone's foot and sprained his ankle severely. He was in pain and had to leave the game. Now for a parent like me, I felt bad for Brody because he was a great inside post player and I don't like to see kids hurt. But with that in mind I was hoping so bad that the coach would give Matt a chance.

That moment got me to stand up and look down at the bench. I saw Coach Litchfield stand up and walk along the bench looking at each player. With a close game and one of our strongest posts hurt he was trying to decide who he could put in the game. I was thinking to myself, "Could this be happening? Will he possibly pick my son to go in for the injured Brody?" He walks over to Matt and taps him on the shoulder. To this day I don't know what he said to him but I know that Matt was shaking his head up and down agreeing with what the coach was saying.

This was his chance to prove that he could contribute to the team. That moment was his turning point where he would take off and contribute more to the JV team. He was still not physically as strong as he needed to be, but he knew the plays well and had developed the fundamentals of blocking out for rebounds. That game he scored some points, pulled down some huge rebounds, and we ended up winning the game. From that moment Matt played at least half of the game the rest of the season.

During the summer, before Matt entered his junior year at McNary High School, he started a weight training program. This kid was serious and on a mission. It is rare these days to see kids as dedicated as Matt. He was working very hard at achieving some of his goals. One of his goals was to become stronger since he would possibly be playing the post position. He would do some running, weights and shooting. He also started taking some protein shakes to help build stronger muscles.

My son put himself on a strict healthy diet. No soda, burgers, fries, or any kind of junk food. He would eat chicken, rice, vegetables and fruits. To drink, he had milk, 100 percent orange juice, protein shakes and water. I was busy going to the grocery store filling his orders. Most of the time he came with me, since he knew what he needed exactly.

Matt had grown two more inches during the summer and now stood at 6'1". He was an inch taller than me now. The struggle he would run into is missing his shots more than usual. Because he was growing so fast, his jump shots and free-throws were starting to seem very flat. So everyday for a few weeks I would hold a broom above my head in front of him, while he tried shooting the ball over the broom. This forced Matt to put more arch on his shot. I think he got tired of me telling him, "The ball will go in more often if it comes down into the rim instead of sideways." We finally corrected that problem and his shots were starting to fall in again, snapping the net instead of hitting the back of the rim first. That problem is pretty normal with kids that grow fast all of a sudden. It is very important that this problem be corrected as soon as possible.

By the time the tryouts started again for Matt's junior year there was no question about whether he was good enough to be on the JV team. But there was a question of whether he would be on the Varsity team or the JV team. Some people felt that Matt could have played varsity basketball that year. But the way things turned out, worked out just fine. Coaches at McNary High School make decisions based on what's best for the basketball program.

The coaches decided to put Matt on the JV team. The JV coach that year was Bob Jones. That was nice because Bob had coached Jake his freshman year. Matt would also swing to varsity and play a few minutes. I feel that's the best scenario for anyone who might be in Matt's situation today. Playing on the JV team he received an enormous amount of playing experience and was one of the starting five. This was a fun year for me to watch my son grow and learn more about the game and also for him to help make the JV team stronger. I was living a dream that his mother and I had for him. She would have been so proud of him and the successful season he was having playing JV basketball his junior year.

TWELVE

SUMMER BEFORE SENIOR YEAR
2002

I DID EVERYTHING I COULD

This was the time that I noticed how much Matt was studying the Bible Scriptures. In the previous years I would give him rides to all sorts of Young Life activities where a youth pastor would lead high school kids in having some good clean fun. Now that he was driving his own car, he would not only attend the Young Life meetings, but also he would attend a Sunday evening Bible study for senior boys at a friend's house. I couldn't have been more proud. It was really nice to see my son having a close relationship with God.

Matt usually worked as a counselor at kid's basketball camps during the summer for a little extra money, and part of the time for a retail store. He dedicated himself to a weightlifting program that he set up on his own. We belonged to an athletic club with all kinds of facilities including a gym. This was Matt's second home where he trained on his own and sometimes with his teammates.

I usually joined him and his teammates when I could. It was fun watching how competitive they all were. What I started hearing pretty regular was a nickname that Matt was somehow given. One of Matt's friends would yell out, "Noza! Are you ready to play some one-on-one?" I guess I didn't really realize it until his high school days.

Jared Wick was probably the kid that worked out with Matt the most. They had been friends since the grade school days. They played one-on-one quite a bit that summer as well as pick up basketball games with others. Countless hours these two spent at the gym. Jared was a competitor and a great one-on-one player. It was fun watching those two play basketball. Jared was quick and he helped Matt improve on his defense. Because of Matt's height now at 6'2" and Jared's height which maybe at the time was 5'7", the rebounding advantage usually went to Matt.

I spent a lot of time with Matt that summer and I was also keeping up with Jake. Jake decided to red-shirt his first year out of high school. The following year he was ready to play college ball. On the day before his recruiting trip to North Seattle Community College in Seattle, Washington, he broke one of his ankles in a pick up game. Later when he healed he was recruited by Linn-Benton Community College in Albany, Oregon. He ended up playing there that year on an athletic scholarship.

Matt and I were very proud of Jake. A son playing college basketball on a scholarship was like a dad's dream come true. I am sure that all the basketball dads out there right now would not disagree with me. It's something that only a few athletes get in life and to have a son that accomplished that was pretty amazing.

I think all parents out there should give their kids a chance. You never know what can come out of hard work and not giving up. With my older son, Jake, who was a college student now, it worked out. He got his tuition paid through basketball.

I think by Jake playing college basketball motivated Matt even more and inspired him to workout even harder to get to where he wanted to be. On a regular basis Matt and Jake would play one-on-one in our backyard. I watched them and tried giving Matt pointers to help him out, but unfortunately that was the age that he probably didn't want to hear from his dad too much, so I cooled it a bit. Jake was taller and more aggressive around the hoop, so Matt took a lot of beating. He would eventually win a few games, but it wasn't easy.

Jake helped Matt get better, he also helped him on how to play defense against someone bigger than him. Blocking out for rebounds was one of the things Matt really worked on. He was going to be one of the shorter posts in the league and he would end up guarding the biggest player on the opposing team. So as you can see his work was cut out for the summer to prepare for his senior year. He had a coach that had a lot of confidence in him. Coach Litchfield was relying on Matt's skills, since he would be the strongest inside player, basketball smart-wise and physically.

Matt knew that the summer league games would soon be over. With plenty of time left before school starting, he wanted to play in something bigger than a summer league. He had gained so much confidence and he had the desire to challenge himself to the highest potential. He wanted to do anything possible that would help him improve for his senior year coming up at McNary High School.

Every year in Oregon there were tryouts for a selected team of age 17 and under kids. The team was called, "Oregon Ice." Matt had tried out for this team when he was 14 years old and when he was 15 years old, but he never made the team. I always looked at it as a good experience and I understood that the tryout would be a big challenge for him. This team was a prestigious team of talented individuals representing Oregon in a National Tournament.

I was surprised when Matt approached me one night that summer and asked me for fifteen dollars to pay for a tryout fee. I asked him, "What team are you trying out for?" He said, "The Oregon Ice, the tryouts are going to be held at Clackamas Community College." I responded, "Good for you! That will be a great experience even if you don't make it."

I gave him the money and the next morning he got in his car and headed to Oregon City, close to where the college was located. In the previous years I had gone with him to watch the tryouts, but this time I told myself to stay home and let him do this on his own. He would be under less pressure and probably feel more comfortable.

When he came back home late in the evening, he said, "Dad I had a great tryout! I hope I made it, they are going to be playing at the Adidas Big Time in Las Vegas." I responded, "Wow! That would be so awesome if you made it." Matt explained to me that he shot well and he did the best he could on all the things that they asked him to do.

The next night we received a call from Coach Craig Rothenberger who was a head coach at Junction City, Oregon. He was one of the coaches taking the all-star team to Vegas. Craig talked to Matt on the phone and said that they would love to have him play on the team. The excitement and joy on Matt's face was priceless. What I was thinking is how much he deserved the good news. After all that he had been through and all his hard work, I was very proud of him for being persistent and reaching a goal he set very high for himself.

Later that night I laid in bed just thinking of how proud his mom would have been if she was still here with us. I would experience many moments like that with all of Matt and Jake's successes. I was proud of both my boys for focusing and hanging in there through life's rough times. I prayed often to the good Lord and felt like he was taking care of us.

An experience that we had during the summer league was a scary one. In two weeks Matt was set to go to his first practice with the Oregon Ice team in July, and in three weeks they were headed to Vegas. Matt was playing his final summer league game against McKay High School. Within four minutes into the game Matt was playing defense and helping on the weak side. The ball was passed across the court to McKay's Trevor Scharer, he took a jump shot and Matt jumped up in an effort to block the shot. He got a piece of the ball, but on his way down he landed on Trevor's foot and fell to the ground. He immediately got up and limped off the court displaying intense pain.

All I could think of is how much he was looking forward to playing with the Oregon Ice team in Vegas. Not only that but he was my son and I felt the pain. He was in tears while trying to walk it off but it was no use, he was really hurt bad. I went down to the bench where he was starting to ice it. The ankle was badly swollen, with blue and black around it. Just knowing my son, for him it was probably more painful thinking about the Vegas tournament coming up.

I helped him as he put his arm around my shoulder and limped next to me as we walked across the gym. Everyone was watching and by their expression I could tell they were really worried for Matt. We left the game early and did not return. I asked Matt if he wanted me to take him to the doctor, he said "No! No! I don't want to go to the doctor! It's just a bad sprain. If I go to the doctor they won't let me play in the tournament."

There were tears coming out of his eyes and he was really hurt. I said to him, "Okay Matt, but you have to promise me that you will stay off that ankle for one week."

He said, "Okay Dad I will." I felt so bad for him and all I could do is just look up and say, "Why Lord? Please give my son some encouragement and give him strength right now."

Just to give you an idea of how tough this kid is, after he sat out for one week he began walking on his ankle slowly. I think the good Lord heard my prayers. The second week he started shooting baskets on it. We taped his ankle for support before his first practice with the Oregon Ice team. We iced it really well after any kind of activity that included using the ankle. I really thought it was just a sprained ankle, but we didn't really know until we returned from the Adidas Big Time Tournament in Vegas.

Before I tell you what happened to the ankle let me first share what Matt did with this injured ankle. Matt was the third leading scorer of the Oregon Ice team averaging 8.8 points and hitting 11 three-pointers during the tournament. It was a fun time and even though Oregon Ice got eliminated after the third game in this tough tournament, we came away with a great experience and something we will always remember.

During one of the games I even got to meet the great LeBron James who now plays for the Cleveland Cavaliers in the NBA. He was sitting next to his team on the bench with a hurt wrist. Matt had told me that this high school player was entering the NBA straight from high school. So I walked down and approached him as he was cheering his team on. There were kids walking up to him asking for autographs. I said to him, "LeBron how is your wrist?" He said, "It's getting better." Then I introduced myself to him, "I'm Dave Espinoza and I have a son playing in this tournament." He said, "Nice!" And finally I said, "Good luck in the NBA." He said, "Thanks man!" He gave me a hand shake in a cool way and I walked away. He was big, about 6' 8" and he was very polite to me.

Now I'll tell you what was wrong with Matt's ankle. The summer was just about over and school was just about to start again. We had to complete a sport's physical for him, so we drove to the doctor's clinic. As I was waiting in the lobby area, the doctor comes out and tells me that she wants to x-ray Matt's ankle, she said it looked a little swollen. So we had his ankle x-rayed. When the results came back it turns out that he had fractured it and played with a fractured ankle at the Adidas Big Time Tournament in Vegas. The doctor said that luckily it had healed right, but she said we should have come in when it happened.

I don't know how Matt played so well at the tournament. His mental toughness certainly played a role. After hearing what the doctor said we were very thankful that he could continue playing basketball.

THIRTEEN

SENIOR YEAR 2002-2003

A 6'4" STARTER ON VARSITY

Matt continued working on quickness drills and lifting weights. When we went to the gym he instructed me on how to assist him during his shooting workout. He would have me pass him the ball as he was running to the planned spots. He would shoot the basketball from the designated spot. These spots were assigned for him to prepare for the upcoming season. Some of these patterns were designed for Matt to get an open shot. He would take inside shots, outside shots and deep three-point shots.

He would say to me, "Dad when you pass me the ball, pass it with some authority!" I would pass him the ball and he would take another shot. The next time he would say, "Dad! A little faster please old man!" We did this through the summer and through the fall. Jake would also come with us to workout. Sometimes I would just watch them workout together.

Matt would even shoot baskets in our backyard until midnight by himself or with a friend at times. One friend that came over now and then was Grayson Boucher, who is now "The Professor" on the And1 Mixtape Tour. He also plays professional basketball in the CBA League. Grayson played basketball with Matt during his junior year on the JV team and swung to the varsity team playing some with Jake. He has always been a good friend of Matt and Jake, and to this day they keep in touch when their schedules allow.

Grayson is one of the best ball handlers I have ever seen. When he was out in the backyard with my boys late at night I felt sorry for the neighbors, they had to hear the boys bouncing the ball and shooting all night long. I didn't help, because I actually purchased some spot lights to give them more light.

Matt had grown from 5'7" as a freshman to 6'4" 210 lbs. as a senior, and was going to be the strongest inside player McNary would have that year. I continued hearing some of Matt's friends using the nickname, Noza.

"What's up Noza?"

"See you later Noza."

"Nice shot Noza!"

That was what some of his friends would say when I was around them. I guess it just sounded easier to say and it eliminated an abundance of letters from Espinoza.

The other senior inside player for McNary was 6'5" Keith McCallister. Keith was probably the team's best shot blocker. He could really hustle and he had long arms, he definitely would play a major role on the varsity basketball team.

I was very excited for this season, I was so excited that I would actually go and watch some of the practices. I would be the only parent there. At least I don't remember anyone else going. I remembered back in the grade school days when all the parents would go watch a practice. In high school that usually didn't happen unless you were a parent like me. It was fun watching Matt work hard at practice with the kids he played with for such a long time through the years. They all worked together and they listened well to Coach Litchfield.

McNary played in the Valley League Conference which consisted of ten of the biggest schools in the state. These schools are, McNary, South Salem, North Salem, West Salem, McKay, Sprague, Corvallis, Crescent Valley, West Albany and South Albany.

I remember the preseason polls in the papers. McNary was ranked fourth in the Valley League Conference. They said McNary just didn't have the size and they lost some key players from last year. I think Matt and all of his teammates knew they were out on a mission and didn't listen to what the papers wrote.

The team had four sharp shooters that were very accurate; Matt, Josh, Robbie and Ryan. Ryan was the quarterback for the football team and had sustained an injury during the last game of the football season. He had a cartilage tear on his knee and sat out for the first few games of the basketball season, this definitely hurt but the team made the adjustment to play without him until his health improved and he was ready to play.

At the time, South Salem, Crescent Valley and West Albany were the power houses with plenty of talented players. That was going to be McNary's challenge and I remember hearing Coach Litchfield talking about Matt having to guard the biggest players.

West Albany had a front line of 6'6" Tyler Roberts, 6'6" Grant Morasci and 6'7" Brian Freeman. South Salem had a post, 6'7"Alex Veit, and one of the best point guards in the Valley League, Jeremiah Dominguez. Crescent Valley had a player who was also a great point guard in the Valley League, Mike Green. Mike had a teammate that was very athletic, 6'4" Keith Hoffman. I guess I would have to say that Matt's blocking out for rebounds became a necessity for him.

McNary also had one of the top point guards in the Valley League, Josh Erickson. Josh was a quick point guard that could shoot the ball, make an assist and defend. When you have a point guard like that with 3 sharp shooters around him like Matt, Robbie and Ryan; that could be very dangerous for defenses.

With all that said, the Valley League Conference also had teams you could not take lightly, Sprague, McKay, Corvallis and South Albany were also teams that could upset any of the top teams on any given night. McNary would not have many easy games this season.

A memory I have of one of Matt's best games his senior year, would have to be against West Salem. West Salem had a kid that was 6'6", Jordan Zeeb. He was assigned to guard Matt that game and it was a lot of fun watching them both go at it. Matt ended up scoring 22 points which was his highest scoring game of the season; he was definitely on fire that game and could not miss.

In the second half of the season the first big challenge was South Salem, a rival school for so many years. There were players on that team that Matt and his teammates played against for years. Players like, Jeremiah Dominguez, Joe Federico and big Alex Veit were all very familiar. McNary knew that this would be a very tough game.

This time they would have Ryan back in action. South Salem drew first blood as Federico hit a big three-point shot early and South Salem's crowd cheered, "We're number one!" Then Robbie came back and hit a basket, then Veit dunked the ball off of a rebound, their crowd again went wild! A near sold out crowd at McNary High School. Both teams were fighting for the number one spot in the Valley League Conference.

The next connection was a three-point shot by Matt off a missed shot. Robbie tipped the ball over to Matt from a rebound. The fans went wild "Nice shot Noza! Yeahhh!" It was so exciting and I had this feeling that we were going to pull away with the victory. We managed to keep a small lead through out the game, but they fought back to catch up. South Salem's Jeremiah was playing a heck of a game he was very quick and was hitting his shots. McNary had to trap him to keep him from penetrating to the middle.

In the third quarter Matt hit some big shots and pulled down some huge rebounds. Ryan, Robbie and Josh also hit some huge three-pointers. Jared and Keith played great as well. With only four seconds left in the game McNary was up by three points. South Salem was in-bounding the ball, it went straight to Jeremiah he split the defense and took a three-point shot for the tie, but it hit the rim and bounced out! Matt grabbed the big rebound and then he was fouled. The crowd went crazy, "Noza! Noza! Noza!" The entire student section rushed the floor thinking the game was over.

Matt had to wait until the court was cleared before taking his two free-throws at the line. Both shots went in swoosh! Nothing but net! Everyone was up on their feet with some roaring cheers for McNary. With one second left South Salem threw a desperation full court shot and missed. Noza and the McNary Celtics had beaten the rival South Salem Saxons in the second half of the season, 64 - 59.

Matt had referenced once through an interview with a reporter about how he could still hear his mom cheering on the sidelines. I remember his mom cheering for him at every game. I can't imagine how difficult that must have been for him. But I think just knowing that his mom really enjoyed watching him play basketball as I did, and by him loving the game so much, gave him motivation to continue and to be as successful as he could possibly be.

Let me step back for just a quick flashback. When Matt and Jake were very little Candi and I took them to Memorial Coliseum for a Portland TrailBlazer's game. The year was 1991 and we got there early enough to walk around the place. We saw that there was a door opened through the back. We managed to find ourselves in the coliseum where there was a person doing maintenance and getting ready for the Blazer game. I asked him if we could take a picture there. He was more than kind and even took the picture of us. As we were waiting for him to snap the picture, Candi looked over at me and said, "David just think, some day our kids could play here." I responded to her, "Candi that would be so neat, it would be amazing to watch our kids play here."

Jake had already played at Memorial Coliseum when he helped his 2001 McNary Celtics go to the OSAA State Championships. He had an excellent tournament performance. On one of his games he had 19 points and 11 rebounds. Matt and I were there watching the entire tournament. Now it was Matt's turn to help his team make it to State at Memorial Coliseum and complete a dream his mom had when she was alive.

There were still some games left in the regular season and the McNary Celtics were not about to get over-confident just because they beat South Salem. West Albany and Crescent Valley were yet to come and they had some of the toughest players in the Valley League Conference.

Against West Albany Matt guarded Grant Morasci a 6'6" power forward that was very athletic and dominant. West Albany was one of the teams that McNary had lost to in the first half of the season. They were a very tough team and ranked number one in the league. McNary knew they would get another chance in the second half of the season. South Salem was another team that McNary lost to in the first half of the season. I remember in that game Matt had the flu, and still played pretty much the whole game, but struggled a bit. McNary didn't have Ryan for the South Salem game they lost. The kids still fought hard and only lost two games the first half of the season.

West Albany came into McNary's house the second round and I think we played one of the best games of the season against them. Winning against South Salem in the second half of the season gave McNary a lot of confidence. I guess after that happened the boys knew they had a legitimate chance to win the Valley League Title.

It was a tough physical game and Matt had his work cut out for him defending Grant Morasci. West Albany's strongest player was struggling a bit with Matt's defense. Matt kept Morasci from driving to the basket and forced him to shoot outside. Those guys were big. Matt hit some key shots and pulled down some big rebounds by boxing out and by playing solid position. When McNary got the ball on offense Matt popped out on the rollout play when Josh passed him the ball. He was at the three-point line and I could hear the crowd roar after he nailed the shot nothing but net, "Noza! Noza! Noza!" It was a very intense game and we managed to come out with a huge victory. The fans stormed the gym after the game which was quite a sight to see. This time they waited until the game was actually over.

McNary was a very quick team and they could shoot the lights out of the ball. The final score was McNary 67 and West Albany 57. The McNary Celtics may have been undersized, but full of heart. They worked together as a team and that definitely overcame their size.

The final tough game of the season for the McNary Celtics was Crescent Valley, the home of Mike Green, Keith Hoffman and Bret Casey. These players gave the Celtics all they could handle. Playing Crescent Valley at their home and getting the victory was an amazing accomplishment going into the final stretch of the season. Matt and his teammates won the game, 60 - 52, disappointing a packed house at Crescent Valley High School.

I remember walking out of the gym and yelling at the team, "We're going to State! We're going to State!" But they knew better, they responded, "Dave, not yet we have a few more games left." Their attitude about taking one game at a time showed great discipline. Matt used to tell me, "Dad we haven't got there yet, we still have some tough teams to play and they aren't going to lay down for us." He was absolutely right. But somehow I had a good feeling that McNary was going to win the Valley League and get an automatic birth to the state championships. If a team placed second they would have to play in the playoffs before the state tournament and risk their opportunity to advance.

On a positive note my instincts were right. McNary won all of the remaining games and became the Valley League Conference Champions with a record of 16 wins and 2 losses. This also included an automatic birth to the OSAA State Tournament at Memorial Coliseum in Portland, Oregon. Believe it or not the two games they lost came after a spaghetti dinner the night before. What a weird coincidence.

Matt had come a long way from almost getting cut as a freshman and as a sophomore, to working hard with weights, quickness drills, shooting baskets until midnight in the summers, eating healthy, keeping his grades up and of course becoming one of the five starters on the boy's varsity basketball team. The improvements that he made were such an inspiration to many of the younger players. I truly believe a lot of them started following his example in working out and spending time getting better for the years to come.

Matt had a lot of faith in God and a lot of heart, and I know that when he lost his mom to brain cancer it must have been very tough to keep going. I think that he found strength within and worked very hard to make his mom and I very proud and to also get a satisfaction of being able to help McNary make it to the OSAA State Championships, just like his older brother Jake did. But most of all he did it for himself.

Matt was also eyeing that someday he could possibly pay for his college education with an athletic or academic scholarship. Coach Litchfield once said, "I call Noza, A Basketball Success Story."

FOURTEEN

MCNARY HEADS TO STATE 2003

MOM'S DREAM COMES TRUE

In the final State polls McNary was ranked number five and heading into the OSAA State Tournament at Memorial Coliseum in Portland, Oregon. The first team they would face was Barlow High School from Gresham, Oregon. The Barlow Bruins had some big boys including Tyler Otis at 6'9" and Jeff Bell at 6'5" 220 lbs. Their point guard, Nick Klinger, was one of the best from his conference.

Matt would be matched up with Jeff Bell, and Malik Parker Hill would be matched up with Tyler Otis. Malik was a young sophomore with great athletic ability, but still young and developing. Josh Erickson would be matched up with Klinger. Robbie and Ryan would pick up the other guards, who were very tough players as well.

I remember at the beginning of the game with a few minutes into the game our point guard Josh, was holding his stomach and asking the coach to pull him out of the game. All I could think was, "Oh no, our point guard is hurt." Without Josh we would be in big trouble, he was our point guard and one of our senior leaders out there.

Jared Wick stepped up to the plate and filled in while Josh was being looked at. To my relief I found out that Josh had gotten really nervous and needed a little break. After a few minutes on the bench he came back into the game and Jared came out. After a break Josh seemed to be fine and into the flow of the game.

Matt contained Jeff Bell, and at times guarded Tyler Otis. It was a tough game and an exciting game to watch. I saw Matt hit two free-throws early in the game. I also heard a loud roar from the crowd as the ball went in hitting nothing but net, "Yeah Noza!" The crowd sounded like a huge train! I felt a great energy inside me and somehow I had a thought that his mom might just be watching from above.

A huge flash went through my head, I saw a little chunky kid that wasn't very quick or very tall and zoomed into the floor way down there and saw a 6'4" athlete that he had become. He was soaking wet, and wearing a number 40 royal blue uniform standing at the free-throw line. It was such an emotional feeling that I almost had tears in my eyes. I just had to be so proud and I felt honored to be his dad. It was nice to be able to witness how my son was helping the McNary Celtics at the State Championships.

The game was a tough battle fought and a tremendous team effort to take down the Barlow Bruins. McNary had beaten Barlow 56 – 46 in the first round of the state championships. Matt ended up with 9 points and 10 rebounds that game with a balanced scoring attack from Josh, Robbie and Ryan.

The next game would be the toughest game McNary would play in the tournament. They were facing perennial power house Jesuit High School from Portland, Oregon. This team had three brothers that were outstanding athletes. The Tarver brothers would be the players that gave McNary a tough challenge. According to Coach Litchfield, because of the traps and press that the Celtics had not run into all season, they lacked in execution and ended up turning the ball over more than they should have.

In this game Matt was left open in the first quarter and he connected on two back-to-back three-pointers. I saw the McNary crowd go crazy! I remember between quarters there was a girl that told someone next to me, "Noza is on fire they need to get him the ball!" A packed Memorial Coliseum and the roars were louder the next time the Celtics scored. There were so many people from the Salem/Keizer area supporting the McNary Celtics everyone wanted to get a piece of the action.

McNary was a team that had not lost a game since the first half of the regular season, and it was crunch time. It was a tough game and the competition level had jumped up. We were playing the number three ranked team in the state. McNary ended up losing to Jesuit 74 – 67. Matt had scored 10 points and added 3 assists, Ryan led the team with 18 points and 7 rebounds. McNary still had a chance to place fourth, but they had to win two more games.

Coach Litchfield was thinking to himself, "How do you talk to these kids and get them up for the next game. They are used to winning." He knew that they were hurt enough. He went into the locker room and said to his team, "We have to find a way to bounce back and mentally prepare ourselves to get ready to play tomorrow. Our goal at the beginning of the year was to play on Saturday, the final day of the tournament, and I think we can do that. With one more win on Friday, we will reach our goal." I thought Jim did a great job talking to the boys who were really down about the loss to Jesuit. It wasn't about yelling at them, but it was about encouraging them and being proud of his team. He also understood how hurt and down they already were.

As weird as this may seem and I am sure it was just coincidental, the team had gone out for spaghetti the night before. For the third time during the season they had lost after a spaghetti dinner. Two games during the regular season and one at state.

It didn't take the Celtics long to bounce back, because on the following night they destroyed South Medford, 62 – 46. Trust me they did not go out for spaghetti the night before. Matt was ready to play his final game of his high school basketball career the next day. The team had reached their goal to play on Saturday at the state tournament. But to win it would be even sweeter.

Southridge High School from Portland, Oregon, would be playing McNary High School from Keizer, Oregon, for the fourth place trophy on Saturday afternoon. This game was a game that tested who was in better shape and who would execute under pressure.

The game was exciting and the Celtics were displaying teamwork, great shooting and great defense. The Celtics had their hands full with Southridge's Troy Beebe, who was outstanding throughout the game, but just wasn't enough for the Celtic attack. McNary plucked the Southridge Skyhawks, 67 – 44, to take the fourth place trophy. Southridge Coach, Dave Immel, said, "There are no excuses, that team played better than we did today." Southridge Post Troy Beebe led all scorers with 16 points.

Josh, Matt and Ryan lead the Celtics. Josh had 14 points and 4 assists, Matt had a double-double scoring 13 points and pulling down 10 rebounds and Ryan had 7 huge assists. Interviews were done by the newspaper after the game.

Final words after the game first from coach Jim Litchfield, "I got the kids together last spring and talked about what we needed to do to improve, and this is really a result of a lot of weightlifting and a lot of work on quickness and shooting. It shows there is a lot of hard work that goes into this."

Erickson's words after the game, "It feels really good taking fourth, people really didn't expect much from us all year and to come out and get fourth really means a lot for us."

Espinoza's words after the game when he was interviewed, "It was the fourth place game and it really came down to who wanted it more, and we really wanted it. When it came down to the fourth quarter and we were only up by eight we had to start creating and finding open shots. We expected to make it to the state tournament, no one really thought we would make it, but we did."

McNary really had no superstars on this 2003 team. The tallest post players were 6'4" and 6'5". But what the McNary Celtics had was a team that worked together with four solid shooters, and the rest were players that understood their roles on the team. The majority of the players played a lot of basketball in the off season. This 2003 team set a record for the best record in school history at 25-3, tied the longest winning streak in the state for 2002-2003 at 16 in a row, and tied the best team record in the state for 2002-2003.

I truly believe to this day, that winners are made not just in the regular season but also in the off season. Matt is a prime example of what someone can be given and what someone can do with what he was given through hard work and dedication. He not only did it on the basketball court but in the classroom as well. I saw it, and to this day I am so amazed at what Matt did during his high school days.

Matt received several awards his senior year in high school. At the sports banquet after the basketball season was over he received two plaques, "The Most Improved Player Award" and the "Spirit of The Team Award." He was selected by coaches to the Valley League All-Conference Team, and he received another plaque along with a nice breakfast for being selected as the "Salem Sports Breakfast

Athlete of The Week." In the academic world he graduated with a 3.96 G.P.A. and he received an academic and athletic scholarship.

I hope that some young kid out there is reading this book and that he or she somehow finds encouragement with these true words. Even if you aren't playing as much as another kid in the early years doesn't mean that you can't improve by working hard and having confidence in yourself. Don't ever let anyone tell you "You can't." It just takes hard work and dedication. And to the parents that might be reading this book, my advice to you, is, support your child in whatever he or she might be interested in. Help your child develop those skills. Your child deserves a chance. Matt got that chance and he took advantage of it and things worked out for him. Because of his effort and the support from his family, he was able to excel.

FIFTEEN

A COLLEGE BASKETBALL SCHOLARSHIP

I DID IT, ON TO THE NEXT LEVEL

After the state tournament, Willamette University, a NAIA Division III college was very interested in Matt, there was a recruiter asking about him at the state tournament. McNary's athletic director, Mike Maghan, came over to me after the last game and said, "Dave, there is a recruiter from Willamette that is very interested in your son." My eyes lit up and I responded, "Really? Wow!" My first thought was, "We'll just wait and see what they say if they call Matt."

Soon after basketball season Matt waited around to see if anyone would lay down an offer for a scholarship to play college basketball somewhere. Willamette University's Head Coach, Gordy James, called Matt and wanted him to join the Willamette Bearcat's Basketball team. The college would only give academic scholarships and not athletic.

Matt qualified with his good score on the SAT and his 3.96 GPA in high school, but would still have to pay thousands more. Most of the players there were on academic scholarships which paid for part of the tuition, but the players would have to pay thousands for the remaining tuition costs and other fees that weren't covered.

Matt knew that we did not have much money, at least not for what Willamette would cost us. It was a very expensive college that specialized in law. We felt really honored that the coach was interested in Matt. Willamette has always had a good basketball program, but I am not sure that the career programs they offered there were of Matt's interest at the time. In addition, the cost was too high for our budget and Matt chose to seek other options.

Linn-Benton Community College is where Jake had just completed his first year. Everett Hartman, one of the assistant coaches, was trying to recruit Matt to play there. He invited Matt to come scrimmage with the team in the spring. Matt did that and I thought, "That would be so awesome if Matt and Jake could play on the same college team together." Unfortunately head coach Randy Falk wanted Matt to be a walk-on. This meant that he would not get a scholarship the first year with a chance that he may get a scholarship the following year.

Matt called Coach Cliff Wagner from Clackamas Community College. Wagner was one of the coaches that took an Oregon all-star team to play in tournaments during the summer. He remembered Matt from the Adidas Big Time tournament in Vegas and how well he shot the three-point shot. He invited Matt to come play with his team in the spring. Matt drove there once a week on Wednesday nights. Wagner kept inviting him again each week, but wasn't offering anything yet.

Matt got on the phone again and started calling more community colleges. This time he was heading out to SWOCC (Southwestern Oregon Community College) in Coos Bay, Oregon. The college was located in the Southern Oregon Coast. I decided to explore the adventure with him this time. We drove almost four hours to get there.

When we got there we drove up to the college and it was raining hard. We finally found the gym. It was a look that I had never seen before. It was a tall white building but nothing fancy. We had to climb up a flight of stairs about one-story high. We walked into the gym and Matt looked tall next to me. Matt was 6'4" and weighed 205 lbs. We met Coach Perkins and some of the players that were going to be scrimmaging.

One of the players was Doron Perkins, last year's player of the year in the NWAACC (Northwest Athletic Association of Community Colleges). He was headed to play at the University of Santa Clara, a Division I school. Coach Perkins matched up Doron with Matt to see how Matt would do. Matt knew how tough Doron was and how he had performed for SWOCC in the past.

Once again Matt had to prove to another coach that he could play college basketball and once again this was his chance. It was fun watching him play against college players. I was really amazed at how the level of competition jumped up a notch from high school. Matt stayed in good shape through the spring and it paid off. He was able to stay with Doron.

Matt scored some baskets on him and played some tough defense even blocking one of Doron's shots. When that happened Coach Joel Perkins looked at me and smiled, "What do I have to do to get your son to play here?" I answered, "Well, I know he has another coach looking at him from Clackamas Community College right now, I think he is exploring his options right now. But you can ask him about that after the scrimmage." I remember him also saying, "Matt's a pretty big kid and he has big time range on his shot. We could really use someone like him."

I really felt good just from listening to the coach and the things he had to say. After the scrimmage was over he showed us some of the campus. The campus was a nice small relaxed environment with a nice walking bridge over a stream where you could see fish. Students use the bridge to walk over to their apartments from the campus. I really liked the college setting there and I think Matt did too.

When we were getting ready to leave the coach walked us out to the car carrying his umbrella to shield himself from the rain. He thanked Matt for coming down and laid down his offer saying, "Matt, I want to offer you a full tuition scholarship with meals to play for the Southwestern Oregon Community College Lakers. We can't pay for your room but sometimes you can work at the college to make that up." Matt responded, "Can I think about it for a few days? I am still playing for another coach and need to talk to him." Joel responded, "Sure that would be fine, but think about it, free education you can't beat that."

On the way back home just from talking to Matt he was sounding like he really wanted to play at SWOCC. He really liked some of the things the coach had to say about him. He knew that he had my support in whatever decision he made. So the only thing left was to see what Cliff Wagner had on his mind at Clackamas Community College. Matt had to make one more trip the following Wednesday.

During the wait Joel Perkins called me up twice that week and sent me a tape of some of the SWOCC games in the past years. I saw how the students would go crazy at their home games. That was pretty cool to see. When Joel called me one evening, I told him that Matt was not home but was leaning toward his program. Joel asked me, "Is he 80 percent leaning toward us or 90 percent?" I said, "I think it's more like 98 percent." He started chuckling a bit, and by the sound, he must have had a smile on his face.

When Matt arrived from Clackamas Community College the next Wednesday evening he looked at me and said, "Dad I think I've decided where I am going." I said, "You have?" He continued, "Southwestern Oregon

Community College." The next day Joel Perkins called us again and this time Matt answered the phone. It was great news for us and for Joel. He mailed Matt a Letter of Intent to sign. He would play basketball in Coos Bay, Oregon, home of the Southwestern Oregon Community College Lakers!

Matt signed to play college basketball for two years on an athletic and academic scholarship. This was a moment that I would remember forever and a memory that our whole family was very proud of. When Matt's brother found out he was very proud and excited for his little brother. This meant that they would play basketball against each other in college and not just in the backyard. Linn-Benton Community College was in the same conference as Southwestern Oregon Community College.

SIXTEEN

FIRST YEAR AT SWOCC 2003-2004

BATTLING MY BROTHER IN COLLEGE

It was summertime once again and Matt didn't seem to want to give his body a rest. He was training harder than ever to get ready for his first college basketball season. Everyday he would complete some kind of a workout whether it was shooting the basketball, lifting weights, or climbing steps at Willamette University Stadium, in Salem, Oregon, where we live. It was very rare that I didn't hear him in the backyard late in the evening shooting baskets. He also had a job on top of all that to earn extra money.

For the first time I would be home alone at the end of August. We helped Matt move his things to his apartment and started getting him settled for a new adventure. Jake would be back at Linn-Benton CC in Albany, Oregon. I guess knowing that they would only be a phone call away or that I would be at their games through the basketball season made me feel a little better.

When Jake and I drove back after saying goodbye to Matt, we stopped in Albany so I could drop him off and say goodbye to him. I gave Jake a hug.

"Take good care of yourself Jake, I love you."

"I love you too. You gonna be okay Dad?"

"Yeah, I'll be okay, I am so proud of you and Matt."

Driving back home was one of the loneliest things I had ever done. It was so quiet, no alternative rock music, no hip-hop music and no conversations between the two boys or me.

I was thinking to myself about the time they both played in that basketball tournament when Matt was in the first grade. It seemed like yesterday and now they were both growing up and gone to college. Where have the years gone? It was very hard for me to let go of my two sons that I had been so close to for so many years. It was very difficult for me to hold the tears back. I remember Matt telling me, "Dad don't worry I'll be back in the summer again." That definitely made me feel a little better.

The days went by and I slowly adjusted to a different life, a life with no kids at home. But with each of them having cell phones, technology couldn't have been nicer to me, because I could call them and talk to them when I needed to hear their voice.

I was very excited for the upcoming basketball season. The first chance I had I called Matt to hear how things were going. He always filled me in on what was happening. Jake was only forty minutes away and he would come home occasionally. He would also fill me in on how his studies and basketball practices were going.

When basketball practices started Matt always updated me on how things were going with the team. I remember him telling me how much tougher practices were in college. He would say to me, "Dad they just run us a lot, I seem to be very tired at night when I do my homework. It's a lot tougher than high school was." He would always tell me about his injuries as well. Thank God for email, it was nice sending him emails when I couldn't reach him by phone.

Matt was practicing with a bruised bone for a week and he did not want to say anything because he was fighting for a starting spot on the team. The coach noticed he was starting to limp at practice. He approached Matt and told him to sit out a few days until he healed up. I was thinking to myself, "A starting spot on a college team?" I would have been so proud of him if he earned some playing time. Matt had improved so much that he had a chance to be a starter. Unfortunately because of the bruised bone on his foot he came off the bench in the first game of the season.

Matt would finally play in his first preseason tournament. It was going to be an exciting one for all of us. I hadn't seen Matt since Jake and I dropped him off at the college in August. It was really nice to see his face again. When he came into the game off the bench, the first thing I noticed is how much better his defense was compared to when he played in high school. He managed to hit 3 exciting three-pointers in the game and finished with 14 points. Not bad for a first official college game he played in.

Matt would become a starter in the second game of that tournament. The coach saw how much he contributed to the team when he was in the game playing. I would say for about 80 percent of the time he was a starter during the season. But it didn't matter to me whether he started or not, I really loved that he was playing a lot of minutes.

Matt was featured on the local Coos Bay news channel on TV. He actually got interviewed for ten minutes. He talked about the team and the good community interaction they had with the people and the young kids at the grade schools. It's a real cool thing to see if you are a parent or know someone that gets that opportunity. It's not everyday that an opportunity like that comes along. Matt did a fine job speaking. In fact he did so well, that the reporter asked him, "Have you ever thought about going into broadcasting as a career?" That was a pretty nice compliment. I still have the tape to that interview and I watch it from time to time.

The first half of the season the Lakers were actually having a winning season and were about to face Jake Espinoza and the Linn-Benton Road Runners. Jake was coming to Coos Bay to battle his brother Matt and the SWOCC Lakers in a college basketball dual. The coaches had never seen opposing brothers in this league.

In a near-packed house the word was out that the two brothers were playing against each other. I kept hearing the people say, "Those two are brothers and they are playing against each other!" It was kind of neat actually to have a good conflict like that. That was a game that I was confused on who to cheer for, so instead I just took a lot of pictures. As I was taking pictures someone asked me, "Who are you going to root for?" I said, "Whoever scores."

During the warm-ups the two brothers were talking a little. Matt's team gave him a hard time, "Hey Noza! Whose side are you on?" Matt just smiled and then went back to the warm-ups with his team.

The time had come for the game to start. After the National Anthem I looked down to the court and saw Matt and Jake, my two sons, walking to the center circle where the jump would take place.

Jumping for the ball to start the game was Bobby Schindler from LBCC and Troy Grey from SWOCC. Matt and Jake were standing side-by-side on the outside of the center circle next to each other awaiting the jump ball. A dad watching his two boys playing college basketball against each other is such a great feeling. I feel really blessed that I was given a wonderful experience like that. Watching this game was not torture for me, but it was the best kind of stress to have, it was like a dream come true. That's how I can best describe it.

During the game Matt would talk to his brother about things that had nothing to do with the game they were playing in. Once at the free-throw line Matt actually said, "Jake did you see that Simpson's episode where Homer worked from home?" Jake would answer back, "Yeah I did, it was pretty funny." That's what some of the conversations were like.

When they were playing they played serious and aggressive. Matt drew first blood by hitting a big three-point shot from way out in the corner. The crowd went wild! "That's it Noza! Show him whose boss!" SWOCC fans were very vocal and loud. The gym was an old echo-type that sounded loud. This was great for a home court advantage.

Jake countered with a nice two-point basket and then an assist to Ryan Schmidt, one of his old teammates from McNary when he played in 2001. The next play Matt was running down on the left side and received a pass from Lionel Denson, the point guard. Matt put up a three-point shot again, this time from the left side. Jake went up to block it but couldn't quite get the block. Matt fell back and the referee blew his whistle and called a foul on Jake as the ball went in! The crowd went crazy! Everyone was on their feet on that one!

Jake looked at the referee and did not agree with the call, "I didn't touch him!" He helped Matt up and they walked over to the free-throw line. Matt made the free-throw and scored a four point play. Jake was shaking his head and kind of smiled.

The game was close but towards the end Lionel Denson of SWOCC picked LBCC's point guard, Michael Brazil, several times and capitalized on the lay-ups. The crowd went crazy! And it was hard to hear in that place. The final score was SWOCC 75 and LBCC 60. Matt would finish with 12 points and 3 assists, and Jake would finish with 6 points, 8 rebounds and 4 assists.

The entire game was exciting to watch and I knew that they would meet one more time in the second half of the season. The brothers were smiling and joking around afterwards. We took some pictures and talked for awhile. I took advantage of that moment since we would not be together like this again for weeks.

I had a moment where I was thinking about the past. I thought about Candi and what she had said to Matt when he was little, "Matt you are always trying to keep up with Jake. Don't get discouraged just because you are short right now and can't stay with him. One day you will be competing evenly with your older brother. Just keep working hard and don't give up." I have to say that witnessing what she predicted was pretty amazing. She was an amazing woman that knew her two boys well. We will always have a great memory of her.

Matt was beginning to have a reputation of the great three-point shooter in the NWAACC. Coaches everywhere would learn right away that he could shoot the three-point shot from way beyond the arc. Head Coach Joel Perkins started setting up plays for Matt to get an open look.

Espinoza was a lot quicker than he was in high school. But defenses would still key on him, and double-team him at times just to not give him a look at the basket. When that happened he would find another player open for an easier basket. He would stretch out defenses and create opportunities for the other players.

Matt was frustrated at times. I remember one game he decided to make something happen off the dribble. He would dribble the ball with his left hand and drive toward the center of the three-point line. He would then fake like he was going to continue dribbling but would stop quickly and release the shot. This would draw the opponent backwards and give Matt an open look.

He started creating plays for himself at times and did very well. Most of the time it was receiving a pass and shooting the three-point shot, or a lay-in off of a play that was executed. He also faked the three-point shot and drew the opponent up in the air while he dribbled to the side and took a good shot. Lionel Denson was one of Matt's friends through that year and they played well together. Lionel usually drove past defenders and when he was double-teamed he would pitch it out to Matt for an open three-point shot.

In Matt's first year of college basketball the Lakers had a chance to go to the NWAACC Championships in 2004, but a string of bad luck took its toll. The last game won by the Lakers was at Umpqua Community College in Roseburg, Oregon, before heading up to Linn-Benton Community College. Matt would face his brother in a dual one more time.

During the Umpqua game Matt was connecting on his three-point shots and on defense, guarding one of Umpqua's biggest players. I guess as a parent the moment I am about to tell you is one that I was really concerned about. It really scared me and I was very worried for Matt. While playing pressure defense on a 6'6" post, Matt frustrated the player. The player swung his elbow hitting Matt on the face. Matt went down and blood started gushing out all over the floor. And to top it off, the official called a foul on Matt, and he was the one bleeding!

I was really furious and could not believe what was happening! I was very concerned as the trainers went out on the court and helped him up. Matt didn't seem like he was doing very well walking back to the bench. When they stopped the bleeding the coach put him back in the game. The next time he was running on a fast break I noticed he was staggering a bit, he received a pass from one of our guards, caught the ball, and took an inside shot. Matt was fouled and went to the free-throw line.

He did not look like he should have been out there. Matt took his first shot and did not even get close. I knew something was wrong. Matt's free-throws were usually pretty automatic. He also missed the next shot as it fell very short of the rim. Coach Perkins took him out of the game. He never returned for the remainder of the second half. It turns out he had received a concussion by the elbow that was thrown. The team had to keep him awake on the way back to Coos Bay. Concussions are a serious injury to the head, I was glad the team was there to help him. He was taken to the doctor the next day. The doctor recommended that he take a week off.

Concussions are not good, it takes the brain awhile to recover and stabilize. I know that Matt would never say anything or make any excuses, so I wasn't surprised when he suited up for the game against his brother a week later. He didn't want to miss that, but was not 100 percent yet.

Linn-Benton played one of their best games ever against the Lakers that day. Matt struggled with his head not being fully recovered from that brutal concussion the week before. That helped Jake and the Linn-Benton Road Runners get a step closer to making it to the NWAACC Championships. There were lots of local people that knew us and went to the game to watch the brothers battle against each other. The local paper had written a huge article, it was a real big deal and I felt honored. The event attracted people from everywhere.

It was a big day for Linn-Benton. 6'7" Ryan Schmidt and 6'5" Jake Espinoza and the rest of the team were clicking in just about every cylinder that game. SWOCC battled tough but it just wasn't their night. The final score was LBCC 79 and SWOCC 69.

In the second battle of the season for the brothers, Matt tallied 9 points, 6 rebounds and 4 steals. Jake scored 4 points, 4 assists and 4 steals.

After the game several people waited to greet Matt and Jake. Jake came out of the locker room first and he was in a really great mood because of their victory. I was happy for him, but had mixed feelings because I knew how bad Matt wanted to go to the NWAACC Championships. My heart felt pulled in two ways, happiness for Jake and compassion for Matt.

I could tell that Matt was very disappointed and also I could tell that he was not fully recovered from the concussion he had suffered at Umpqua. But just knowing him, he was going to play in this game against his brother no matter what. Sitting out a week before playing a hard game is not easy to do, but he did it at maybe 70 percent.

There were a lot of parents and friends from the high school days that came to watch the brothers play against each other. Some of my relatives that I hadn't seen in a long time also came to watch the game, the gym was packed.

I was thinking to myself as I was waiting for Matt to exit the locker room down this long hallway, "I know that Jake's team could possibly make it to the NWAACC Tournament this year, and this year would be his only opportunity. Matt would have another chance next year if it didn't work out for him this year." I think those thoughts made me feel a little better, but to tell you the truth I just don't know what would have made me feel better. It was a tough position to be in. I felt great about both my boys not getting injured during the game.

Matt was walking very slowly down the long hallway from the dressing room wearing his team cap on slightly to the right. He was probably the last person out of there. I gave him a hug and said, "Matt I am so proud of you, its okay. I am so sorry about the concussion you got. I have been praying for you." Matt had tears in his eyes and I could see his disappointment.

My thinking is that he felt bad because he couldn't help his team more, because of him not being 100 percent yet. And all the people that came to watch him play had no idea what had happened to him the week before. I walked Matt to the SWOCC team bus, put my hand on his shoulder and said goodbye before he headed south for Coos Bay.

To tell you the truth, except for the concussion, I felt it ended well with each son winning one game. My two boys actually got along very well and didn't hold any kind of grudges after those games. I feel very lucky to have experienced watching them play against each other in college and I feel very blessed. When I arrived back home I got on my knees and thanked the good Lord for allowing me to be their dad.

Matt's first year of playing college basketball would be coming to an end. SWOCC did not make the playoffs, losing their two final games. Jake and the LBCC Road Runners won their final two games and advanced to the NWAACC Tournament. Matt and I drove there to watch his brother and root for him.

It was an amazing experience and Matt was in good spirits and already looking forward to the next year. He really wanted to help his team make it to the NWAACC Tournament in Kennewick, Washington. I couldn't have agreed more.

SEVENTEEN

SECOND YEAR IN COLLEGE
2004-2005

A LEADER ON THE COURT

After a summer of college basketball summer league games, training and working to save money, Matt left home for college in August. He had a new job that would pay for his room and board, and basketball would pay for his full tuition. The job he got was primarily due to him showing how responsible he was, and from the staff having a great deal of trust in him. I was very proud of him for accomplishing that on his own.

Matt was a Residence Assistant at the college. He was to help the incoming students with their housing questions and to help them settle in. He would also provide a tour of the college campus to some of the first year students. Through the year he would also carry out his duties as a Campus Monitor every other weekend.

He shared these duties with other second-year students as well. This is the child that saved me a whole ton of money. He maintained a 3.9 GPA, played on a basketball scholarship and worked every other weekend to cover his room and board.

Matt was well-known there at the college. He made several friends and he seemed to be enjoying the college days at SWOCC. His brother Jake was headed to the University of Oregon, to study Journalism and Graphics Design. Jake was also spending a lot of time recording hip-hop music. His dream was to become a Hip-Hop recording artist.

His artist name would be "The Kid Espi" and he was becoming very popular in the local area doing live hip-hop shows. He was working on his first full-length album "The First Book" at the time and writing his own lyrics. He now has another full-length solo album titled, "True Love + High Adventure." If you haven't bought it yet, I encourage you to buy it, it is awesome!

Jake had opportunities to play at a Division II or Division III College, but he had a passion for music and writing. That is what he decided to pursue. I know that he enjoyed playing basketball and he did get two years of college paid through basketball. But it wasn't what he wanted to continue doing, I have a lot of respect for the son I created first and I supported his decision.

Matt was the healthiest I had seen in a long while when he started his second year at Southwestern Oregon Community College. Basketball season was here once again, if you are a basketball fan or a player like I am, the sound of the basketballs bouncing or the sneakers squeaking will make your eyes light up! In my opinion, basketball is the most exciting sport to watch. It is constantly going with very little delays and the crowd's excitement adds to it as well. The athleticism in this sport is the best in the world!

While being alone with no kids in the house I decided to start dating again in hopes that there might be someone special out there for me. I met Loni, a wonderful lady that loved the exciting game of basketball as much as I did. She played basketball in her younger days just like I did, and she had two daughters, Darci and Kalin. She was a single parent just like me and we had plenty of things in common.

I told Matt about her and he was very happy for me, he knew that I would have someone to spend time with and not be alone. He knew who Darci was from McNary High School, since she also attended that school and played basketball there on the girl's team. Her older daughter Kalin graduated high school with Jake.

It was once again time for another year of basketball except this time Loni and I would be at Matt's games to watch. For a regular season home game we would leave Salem right after work and arrive at the game a few minutes before tip-off time. After the game we would drive back to Salem and return about 1:00 A.M. in the morning. You can imagine how fun it was waking up for work in the morning. Matt's Grandmother, Elaine, would also ride along at times. The away games were closer, since most of the colleges were close to the Portland/Salem area.

Once again the first game of the year was a battle for a starting spot on the team. For some reason Matt did not start. Joel Perkins had recruited some really quick wings, 6'1" Jerrod Dastrup and 6'3" Masevai Davis. He also recruited two posts, 6'6" Kurtis Devon and 6'8" David Timpe. The posts were big but not very quick and not as dominating as some in the league. This year once again Matt had to earn his spot, but that didn't take long with his outside shooting and team ball playing.

I remember one of the Lakers' tournaments at the beginning of the year near Sacramento, California. It took place in Elk Grove, California, at Consumes River College on December of 2004. I flew into Sacramento International Airport assuming the college was nearby. To my surprise I arrived at the airport and found out it was fifty miles to Elk Grove. I had already jumped into the taxi when I found out.

The taxi cab driver dropped me off at the college and from there I was able to get a ride from one of the college professors. He was kind enough to show me where the hotels were and to give me a ride there too. The hotels happened to be about four miles from the college and I did not rent a car.

Riding the city bus to the games and back was an exciting adventure. After the first game I had a chance to talk to Matt for a bit before he loaded up the bus and headed back to the hotel, where the team was staying in Sacramento. I then walked over to the city bus stop on the college campus and waited for the city bus. It was so cold that night, and I hadn't eaten anything all day. I felt like I was starving.

Finally the bus came by and I hopped on. I'm the type of person that has to know everything is right. I also ask questions if I'm not sure of something. I asked the bus driver about five questions and he was starting to get irritated. I just wanted to be sure he knew what I was asking.

One of the questions I asked was, "Sir, do I ring the bell before the street I want to stop at or when I see the street?" I let him know the name of the street and his answer was, "Yes." He wasn't listening to what I was asking. Anyway, to make a long story short he got upset with me and dropped me off at the wrong street.

Like I said before it was cold and I was hungry. I had to walk about five miles before I actually found my hotel. I definitely feel for the homeless people in cold weather, it was not fun at all. I managed to find my way back and I laughed about it afterwards. That was a good learning experience and from that point on I always did research before going to games in unfamiliar territory.

On the second day of the tournament SWOCC was playing Feather River Community College, one of the local Colleges. This team had a very athletic group of players mostly from California. They had a couple of players that were headed to play Division I basketball the next year, 6'10" Anthony Washington and 6'9" Brock Richards. Little did we know what was about to happen this game.

The game started out by Feather River's Anthony Washington dominating the boards and dunking on us several times on the fast break. SWOCC was not executing well due to Feather River's tough press. We were having a tough time getting people open for shots. Coach Joel Perkins was frustrated and knew his team had their hands full with this team.

In the second half we were down by about 20 points. I had seen Matt get on these zones several times in the past, not just in official games but in pick up games as well. I guess some people call it, going unconscious. He basically got in a zone and could not miss a shot! It was the game that was worth flying there and walking 5 miles in the cold weather for. I witnessed one of the best college basketball moments Matt would have.

Matt started shooting the basketball over the defender. Brandon Thompson was our point guard with amazing quickness and speed. He was dribbling down with the defender right on his face, Matt popped out on the left side deep in three-point land. Brandon passed him the ball and Matt put it up, nothing but net!

The next sequence Feather River was pressing and Matt was open running along the sideline. Once again he received the ball and off the dribble he took a deep three, this one from NBA range, it glided through the air and went straight in off the back of the rim. This is no joke! I am not making this up. Matt ended up hitting seven three-point shots that game and also tallying his career high of 28 points. He brought his team within four points of tying the game, but it wasn't enough and they ended up losing.

This moment of a personal record for him was really the result of great work that his teammates did to allow that to happen. They were looking for him and getting him the ball. It was as if his teammates were feeling what the crowd was feeling, even the home crowd was cheering when he made one three, and another three, until he had made seven, it was just electrifying!

I knew that Matt would be disappointed if they lost, despite the fact that he hit a career high. To him it was more important to win the game than to score 28 points. That's just the type of person he is.

With seconds left in the game Matt went up for a rebound and landed on one of the opponent's foot. He sprained his ankle really bad and had to sit the rest of the game and ice the injury. Thank God he was able to walk on it afterwards.

We had no idea there were some recruiters there to watch some of the Feather River players. This is what you call being at the right place at the right time. They saw how Matt hit the three-point shot.

After the game Matt was coming out of the locker room limping a little, I was glad to see he was walking. As a dad I would hope I could go give him a hug and say, "What a great game you played son!" Unfortunately, I had to take a ticket because of all the people that stopped him on the way.

The media and two recruiters talked to him for awhile. One of the recruiters found out that I was Matt's dad. He came over to introduce himself. He told me about Cal State-Maritime in Vallejo, California. He really wanted Matt to go there next year, and he would offer a full ride. There was another recruiter there but he didn't know I was Matt's dad, so I didn't get to talk to him.

Matt started walking towards me and one of the Feather River players came up to him. His expression was of concern.

"Hey number fifty! Is your ankle alright?"

"Yeah, it's just a little sore."

"You got a nice game."

"Thanks."

"Where did you learn to shoot like that?"

"Oh, I don't know, I just practice a lot."

In my opinion, every great three-point shooter will have days like Matt did against Feather River Community College. Days like that are a lot of fun, but with that in mind, three-point shooters also have bad days where they just can't hit anything. Luckily, Matt didn't experience too many of those throughout his college basketball career.

At the beginning of the season Matt was averaging about 21 points a game. I remember at another tournament in Seattle, Washington, SWOCC was playing Olympic Community College. This was right before the Christmas break. Matt scored 23 points including seven three-pointers before one of the opponent players accidentally kicked him on the calf muscle.

We managed to win the game in overtime but Matt's calf muscle would be bruised up pretty bad. That night at the hotel he could not bend his leg. Once again he was banged up and I was worried for him. We iced his calf muscle and he took some Advil.

The next morning the team headed back to the tournament where SWOCC would be playing Spokane Community College, a team that one of his old teammates played on. Mitch Grove, a 6'8" post, who played on the Oregon Ice team with Matt back in the high school days.

Matt really wanted to play in this game against his old teammate. He had his calf muscle taped up by the trainer and he was going to try to play. I could tell from watching him in the warm-ups that he was not well. He was limping and in pain as he jogged to the basket during warm-ups. I wasn't about to let him play on an injured leg. All I could think was, "He could cause further damage and possibly end his season."

So I went down to the floor and yelled at him, "Matt! Come here!" He walked over to where I was. I continued, "You're not playing today, you can't even jog on that leg." I could tell he wanted to play so bad the way he looked at me in an angry way, "I have to try at least!" I said, "Matt, you still have the whole season ahead of you, don't make that injury worse." He just looked at me and went back to the warm-ups.

I went back up to the stands and I knew that he would make the right decision. The coaches really wanted him to play, but I told him it wasn't worth it. I was more concerned about him getting well.

As I was watching him I felt bad for him, he was doing so well in this tournament and his team needed him for this game. Matt sat out of the game, and even though we lost, I know that he made the right decision to sit out, I was very proud of him.

During the tournament there was a recruiter from Montana watching. A recruiter from Rocky Mountain College expressed strong interest in Matt. He came over to where I was sitting and started asking me all kinds of questions about Matt. One of his first questions was, "What are Matt's grades like?" I answered, "He has a 3.96 GPA."

He looked at me and started telling me about their basketball program and how Matt could get a full ride playing there next year. He wanted to talk to Matt after the game and wanted to see if he could convince Matt to enroll there next year.

Matt was able to talk to him for awhile. He was a really nice man in his later 60's wearing glasses and spoke very proper. It sounded like Rocky Mountain College in Montana could use a shooter like Matt. He said they really needed a three-point shooter for next year. He added that he would have his full tuition paid for and his room. They usually gave athletes jobs on campus to cover meals. That sounded pretty darn good, but Matt wanted to keep his options open and see who else might offer something.

As the season got going Matt would play with his calf muscle padded and taped to protect the deep bruise. This would prevent any further injury if he got hit again. He always had his ankles taped since he had sprained them a few times.

Matt managed to continue to score well in the next few games, but couldn't move as quickly as he would have liked to. The coaches played him as much as possible with his leg taped up, simply because he was shooting extremely well.

He made some good friends in his second year at SWOCC. I would say that one of his best friends there was Barry Henderson. Barry is from Florida and had tried out for the team but fell short of making the team. He ended up attending school at SWOCC and spending his time as an assistant coach to Joel Perkins.

Matt also had some girls that were his friends, Rosanne Curtis, Anita Curtis and Amy Chapman. There were others, but these I think were his closest friends. The girls played basketball for the women's team which made it fun on road trips and after games. When I traveled to Coos Bay for weekend games I would join them for church on Sunday morning. Definitely some fun times in Coos Bay.

Matt would help elementary kids with their reading once a week when his schedule allowed. He also volunteered at some kid's basketball camps for the Boys and Girls Club. He was the Vice-President of the student body and very involved in all kinds of student activities at the college.

Several times he would take the lead in activities, like setting up barbeques for all the students. He would definitely draw a crowd of students from the college apartments all around. Barry would play the music. He was a DJ and was working all of the sound equipment. Matt was the barbeque cook for all the students. Loni and I helped him get all of the supplies for a barbeque one time. The adventure was a lot of fun.

As the season progressed Matt was playing a lot of minutes, sometimes the entire game. He was becoming a leader out on the floor and I could see that Coach Joel Perkins had a lot of confidence in him. He hardly had any turnovers in his games and his passes were very accurate. I started getting letters in the mail from several universities that wanted Matt to play for them after the junior college years.

During the season Joel Perkins had talked to coaches at SOU (Southern Oregon University) a NAIA Div II college. He had informed them about Matt and how well he shot the three-point shot. Joel also asked them to come watch some of Matt's games.

I had seen one of the SOU assistant coaches at a home game. Anthony Levretz pulled Matt over after one of the games and talked to him for awhile. He said Southern Oregon University had one slot open for a shooting guard. He also said he liked the way Matt shot the ball and how well he was doing academically.

Umpqua Community College was a college that was two hours away from Ashland, Oregon, where SOU was located. The assistant coach from SOU, Anthony Levretz, came once again with another coach this time to watch Matt play against Umpqua Community College.

Matt played a great game hitting four three-pointers and scoring a total of 17 points. One of the three-pointers was beyond NBA range. I just looked over at the recruiters and enjoyed watching the reaction on their faces. They were going to need another three-point shooter at SOU, and it seemed like Matt was a possibility.

I was really impressed with Matt, he had worked so hard to put himself in a position that NAIA Div II and NCAA Div II schools wanted him to play for them. But first he had to finish out the great season he was having for SWOCC.

Matt's team was in the running for a playoff spot and he did not want to think about where he would play next year. The top four teams in the southern division would make it to the NWAACC Tournament in Kennewick, Washington. It was a big time championship tournament of community colleges. We knew there would be all kinds of recruiters there as well.

In the NWAACC conference word had gotten out early in the season that Espinoza could shoot the lights out of the ball beyond the arc. So all season long Joel Perkins had his work cut out for him. I could see his frustration, he had one of the best three-point shooters in the league but was having problems with teams keying on him and not giving him a look at the basket.

I was really impressed when he came up with some plays that gave Matt a two second look, just enough time for him to release the ball and nail a shot. When Matt came to play at the local colleges around the Salem area, coaches knew him well, they would put their quickest defender on him. This would include coaches like David Abderhalden from Chemeketa Community College and Gordy James from Willamette University.

Most of the coaches would make an effort to keep Matt from shooting the three-point shot. Matt learned how to create a three-point shot with someone guarding him close. With some teams, there was just no other way. And sometimes Matt would just pass the ball and not take a shot, which happened several games throughout his college career.

There were times when Matt drove to the basket and dished off a nice pass, or he spread the defense so much that his teammates had opportunities to score easy baskets. Not only that but it prepared him for the future years ahead at a bigger division school.

SWOCC was in third place for most of the season then they dropped to fourth place after losing two close games, one to Clackamas CC and the other to Mt. Hood Community College.

The two top teams were Chemeketa CC and Mt. Hood CC, Clackamas CC was right behind them in third. The funny thing is that SWOCC lost some games in overtime and other games by one point or two points. They easily could have been one of the top teams.

After the last game of the season SWOCC would advance to the NWAACC Tournament capturing the final playoff spot of the league and earning a trip to Kennewick, Washington. Matt felt really great about the team's accomplishment. I think what he wasn't too happy about was losing the close games. Because of those losses they would have to face a top-ranked team in the first game of the tournament.

First Matt's brother went to state in high school, and then Matt goes to state in high school. Next Jake goes to the NWAACC Championship Tournament in college, and now Matt is going to the NWAACC Championship Tournament. I don't know how that happened but I'm sure glad it did. And both times the games were a blast.

The interesting thing is that both brothers faced the same team and won in the tournament. Big Bend Community College from Moses Lake, Washington, was the team that Linn-Benton CC faced the first round of the tournament and they won. SWOCC faced Big Bend CC the following year in the second game of the tournament and won. Both of the games were upsets since both times Big Bend CC was the favorite with a top seeding.

The next day of the tournament SWOCC was eliminated losing to rival Chemeketa Community College. It was very disappointing to Matt and the Southwestern Oregon Community College Lakers. His two years of community college basketball had come to an end and I know he would have loved to advance further in the tournament, but things just didn't workout that way.

I felt bad for him but at the same time I was very proud of him and what he had accomplished. I was waiting for him to come out of the Kennewick Coliseum through the back where the teams would walk out. As he walked toward me with tears running down his eyes, naturally my eyes would start to water as well.

I walked up to Matt and said, "Matt, I am so proud of you and I love you very much. You did an amazing job you have nothing to feel bad about. You helped your team make it here." He responded, "Thanks Dad, I love you too, thanks for everything."

As I walked away toward our car on the parking lot Matt comes out of the bus, "Dad! Wait." He was running over to where I was. He was carrying his basketball shoes, "These are yours." I said, "Thanks Matt have a safe trip back, I'll talk to you soon."

When he gave me his shoes I felt that he was telling me that he appreciated all of the support I had given him throughout his basketball career. To a dad that means so much, or at least to me it did.

Concluding his second year of college, Matt averaged 17 points a game surpassing his high school mark of 8 points a game. He was named to the South NWAACC All-Star Team, which would play against the North NWAACC

All-Star Team. Matt also received a prestigious award, the Scholar Athlete of The Year Award.

During warm-ups at the all-star game most of the players were dunking the ball. Matt was never one to dunk the ball just to show off. But there were some fans that kept asking him to dunk it because they had never seen him dunk before. They would yell out, "Dunk it Noza! Can you even dunk?" That was the first time I saw Matt throw it down during a warm-up. He joined the rest of the South All-Stars and had some fun with it. The last time I saw him dunk the ball was at the athletic club in Salem, his hometown. The all-star game clenched a great season, and it was a real pleasure seeing his smile.

I sure felt blessed and very lucky to have a son like Matt. I had to take a look back at all those years of watching him grow up and being persistent. He worked so hard and was determined to be successful and like Jim Litchfield said, "He was not going to be denied."

I truly hope that a basketball player with a dream like Matt's is reading this book and that he or she realizes that they too can be successful through hard work, dedication, confidence, faith and believing that it can happen.

EIGHTEEN

NAIA DIVISION II BASKETBALL

NOZA PLAYS AT A UNIVERSITY

During the spring of 2005 Espinoza was exploring his options of which university he would play basketball for next season. Some of the colleges that were very interested were; Rocky Mountain College in Montana, Cal State-Maritime in Vallejo California, Cal Baptist, Southern Oregon University, Willamette University in Oregon, Cascade University in Oregon, South Dakota Tech, Oregon Institute of Technology and Western Oregon University.

Phone calls and talks would start for a basketball player who years ago, no one would even think could possibly play college basketball. Back in the grade school, Jr. high and high school days no one would have guessed what was about to happen. I remember talking to some parents that used to go watch the high school games. I once talked to one of the dads. I said to this person, "I've been working with both my boys since they were really little. I am hoping they will play college basketball some day." He looked at me, "That is every dad's dream and very unlikely. Just enjoy his high school games while they last, very few kids get to play college ball."

My thoughts were not like his. I didn't respond to what he said, I just smiled. But inside I totally disagreed with him. You see not many people are like me. I put a lot of work and time into my two boys and acknowledged their gifts. I knew what they were possibly capable of when given the support and the chance. To this day, I truly believe that my prayers were answered.

I feel bad for kids that were college bound and encountered a career ending injury in high school. They never get an opportunity to play college ball. I knew there was a risk, but I also knew that if it was God's will Matt would play college ball after high school. I had faith, I prayed through his high school days for his safety and for him to do well.

Now the day had come for him to play at a university. Matt would talk to several coaches that were interested in him. I could tell that he was looking for my approval for which college he should go to. He pretty much had his pick from the colleges I listed above in an earlier paragraph. They all wanted the shooter people talked about and wrote about in the NWAACC conference.

I knew that Rocky Mountain College would provide him with practically a full ride, and that he would fit in well with their program. I would not make it to very many games and that would be frustrating. I didn't tell Matt what I was thinking because I wanted him to make that decision on his own.

What I told Matt was, "Take me out of the picture, and just go where you fit in with the program, you have to feel comfortable. I want you to be happy with the decision you make, you're the one that will be there not me." I think that helped him not worry about where I wanted him to go. I would be happy for him no matter where he chose.

Matt talked to Coach Jim Boutin from Western Oregon University, Gordy James from Willamette University, Bill Dreikosen from Rocky Mountain College, Matt GreenLeaf from Cascade University, and Brian McDermott from Southern Oregon University.

Finally it was the recruiting trip to Southern Oregon University that really caught Matt's attention. Southern Oregon was a college that Matt really liked after spending a day there talking to Head Coach Brian McDermott and Assistant Coach Anthony Levretz. They showed him around and made him feel needed there. They also told him about the winning team he would be playing with.

They had some returning players for the upcoming season and they had lost a shooter. Two key players returning were 6' 7" Shea Washington and 6' 8" Jeff Williams. SOU coaches were hoping Matt could replace the shooting guard that graduated. This would help Southern Oregon make a run at the NAIA Division II National Championship in Point Lookout, Missouri.

Shea Washington was a monster player that had transferred from Montana State to SOU two years previous. He would be playing his last year at SOU. This player was a dominating force in the inside and was averaging 20.8 points and 10 rebounds for SOU. One of Shea's friends, Steve Farley, was the point guard. Shea and Steve played ball together at Thurston High School in Eugene, Oregon.

Jeff Williams was another scorer that was returning for his senior year as well. Jeff was another player that transferred to SOU in the previous year. Jeff was averaging 9.8 points and 7.3 rebounds per game. His presence on the court was part of the reason the team was so successful. Jeff went to high school at North Salem High in Salem, Oregon, and played against Matt's older brother, Jake, in 2001.

Matt also had in the back of his mind that one of his high school friends was living in Ashland where SOU was located. Jared Wick was a walk-on for the SOU football team two years previous. He broke his ankle in a wakeboarding accident and ended his college football career but continued to get his education there. Jared was a good friend of Matt and they could possibly be roommates in college.

With all the information Matt had been gathering about all the different colleges and players on the teams, it came down to two colleges, Southern Oregon University and Rocky Mountain College in Montana. Rocky Mountain College is where he had already applied to attend college but had not signed anything.

After the trip to SOU he realized he wanted to play on a team that would have a shot at making it to the NAIA National Championships in Point Lookout, Missouri. He wanted to hopefully be a part of that exciting adventure. All the facts that I just mentioned to you was what influenced Matt to select Southern Oregon University.

Matt called me up and told me that he would be signing with SOU. I was really excited and yelled out, "Congratulations Matt! Wow!" He continued, "Dad, you really don't need to drive all the way here for the signing, we will take pictures." I said, "Sounds good Matt, I am so proud of you, you made a great decision."

Matt called Coach Brian McDermott and informed him of the decision he had made. The next thing you know some of the coaches from SOU traveled to Coos Bay to meet Matt. He signed a Letter of Intent to play basketball at Southern Oregon University on a full tuition scholarship.

So it was settled and Matt would officially be a Southern Oregon University Raider the following year. This was great because the college was only four hours away from Salem where we lived. I would be able to drive to all his games.

The rest of the college year at SWOCC would be relaxing for him and he would recover from some of his nagging ankle injuries that came and went. Matt would not have to think about where he was headed next year. He had the opportunity to do some hiking in the coastal range, barbequing and other fun activities with his friends. He continued to play pick up basketball games and lift weights to stay in shape. It was a good change of pace for him and with all his school work and his job he stayed really busy.

The college year had ended and Matt was one of the last students to leave since he was the Residence Assistant. We helped him bring some items back home one weekend. It was really nice seeing him again since it had been awhile. I felt great knowing that he was going to be home again for the summer.

During the summer Matt would go to work again playing in the summer college league and continuing to lift weights. He would also follow through on a workout program that SOU coaches wanted him to do to get in good shape. When you play college basketball you are expected to be in shape when the season starts again.

College is not like high school where most kids get in shape at the beginning of the season. In college if you're not in shape when the first day of practice comes around, your body will pay for it. You also risk a chance of possibly getting cut from the team.

Matt's work ethic allowed him to meet the expectations the coaches had for him. I bought Matt a summer pass to the athletic club so he could train there. He also worked at basketball camps and at a retail store for a little extra money.

Late at night he would shoot baskets in our backyard hoop until midnight. I often turned on the spotlights for him so he could see the goal. Sometimes he would have a few friends over to shoot baskets with him while they talked basketball.

I'll tell you one thing, all the money that I invested in my backyard basketball court and goal has really been worth it. To this day it gets used pretty regular, especially in the summers. I cannot justify going on an overseas vacation or a cruise somewhere, but building something solid we can use for a very long time in our backyard, I can certainly justify.

The vacations can wait for a later time, and I am not speaking for anyone else. My priorities were my two boys and developing them and giving them a place to play that was safe and private. Matt could focus on his shot and on improving his consistency. He loved the fact that no one in the neighborhood would come distract him.

Before I built any kind of hoop, I remembered seeing a cul-de-sac with a large group of kids playing on one hoop. That was good for having fun and playing street games, but that is not what I wanted for my kids. I wanted them to be able to step out of our back door to use the facilities instantly and focus on shot after shot.

When we have barbeques we play all kinds of games. Games like Bump, Horse and Around the World. My relatives that come over always seem to have a blast shooting baskets outdoors with us. A covered basketball court would have been amazing, but my budget could not afford that, and Matt didn't mind shooting in the rain at times.

Let's go back on a flashback story about Matt that really caught my attention. It was during his high school days where he was playing in a basketball game. His free-throw percentage was not too good that day. Normally he would shoot at least 85 to 90 percent, that day he was off a little. I think he shot like 65 percent which was not acceptable to him. When we got home after the game, he put on his hooded sweatshirt and grabbed the basketball. He started heading out to the back, I looked at him and said, "Matt where are you going? It's raining out there." He responded, "I'm practicing my free-throws."

I watched him shoot free-throws in the rain for awhile. Now most parents would probably yell at their kids and make them come back inside the house. I'm different than most parents as my kids can probably tell you. I put on my raincoat, stepped outside, and rebounded for him for the next hour or so. He started making them consistently in the rain.

Anyway the point is that Matt knew he needed to maintain his free-throw accuracy and he would react immediately to fixing what the problem was. I saw it and he never really explained to me what he was doing. He really didn't need to because he demonstrated it so well. Matt was preparing himself for the future basketball career.

Playing college basketball is full of challenging experiences. Not only is it hard to keep up with practices, pressures that go along with team meetings, and performing in basketball games, but it is also very difficult to keep the grades up. You must work on developing good study habits.

Sometimes when athletes travel to play in an away game they ride on the bus for eight hours, round trip would be sixteen hours. And while most of you would think traveling is fun, well, not so much fun when you have to study on the bus or at the hotel. Matt had to do that for four years while playing college basketball.

It was once again time for Matt to pack up his car and head out to his new college hometown, Ashland, Oregon. This town is the home of the Oregon Shakespeare Festival, with plenty of cultural opportunities, music, comedy, experimental theatre and dining. Ashland also has Lithia Park, a National Historic Site. It is called the "Jewel of Ashland." The park is one hundred acres in size with mature trees and beautiful trails. Matt would be attending college in a tourist attraction town.

This time he would leave in August to train with Shea Washington. He got to know Shea and they were the first two players to workout before the actual season started. They worked hard on weights, quickness drills, shooting and plenty of running.

Matt would move in with Jared Wick, one of his friends from the high school days. They shared an apartment that was within walking distance to the college. Jared was a good kid and I couldn't think of anyone else I would rather have him share an apartment with in Ashland. I knew Jared's parents Dave and Judi Wick. I think the arrangement Matt set up was the best one for him at the time.

NINETEEN

SOU RAIDERS 2005-2006

NAIA DIVISION II NATIONALS

It was a new season and the practices were tough at SOU, but the coach I think understood that the kids needed the rest in order to be able to play strong. His practice method was different than most coaches. Most of the coaches that I knew practiced five days a week and some even would go on Saturday.

Brian McDermott would set up practices to rest one day after every three days of practice. This gave the players the rest they needed. I really liked that schedule as it gave the players a chance to rest their muscles. I always thought that colleges work the kids too hard. In my opinion that's one of the reasons some of the injuries occur.

I called Matt pretty regular to see how he was doing. I asked him if he felt he was going to get some playing time when the season started. He always sounded very confident but always very honest. I would ask him, "Matt how are things going? Do you think you will get a lot of playing time?" He would say, "I don't know Dad it's pretty tough, we have some big guys and some really quick guys on our team. I think we're all fighting for a spot."

Coach McDermott recruited a post that was fighting for a starting spot, 6'7" Erion Moore II from East Palo Alto, California. This would help Shea Washington and Jeff Williams underneath the basket. Erion had transferred to play at SOU. Also fighting for a starting spot was 6' 3" RaShawn McAllister from Riverside, California.

RaShawn was a returning player and a very athletic kid that was fast and could dunk the ball easily for his height. Matt was 6'4" and not as quick as RaShawn but could shoot the three-point shot very well. I could see Matt sharing the floor with RaShawn as far as playing time. This year, Matt would be playing the wing position at SOU.

There was another reserve player returning, Matt Cowell. He was a 6'3" wing from Grants Pass, Oregon. Cowell could shoot the three-point shot well and he was a great hustler. So as you can see Espinoza's work was cut out for him.

Coming in new to this program Matt would have to learn the offense and defense that SOU ran. He spent countless hours of making the necessary adjustments. It was nice because he had someone to help him with quickness and defense techniques. Anthony Levretz, one of the assistant coaches, worked with Matt for days helping him with quickness drills.

Coach Brian McDermott spoke highly of Matt at the beginning of the season. In one of his interviews he said, "Matt is a perimeter shooter with big-time range. He's a tremendous worker whose presence will make it difficult for teams to double-team our inside players." That was such a nice compliment and acknowledgement of what Matt could do.

In another interview McDermott said, "I believe that 6'4" Espinoza will become the purest 3-point shooter of my coaching tenure. He's so efficient with the ball he never forces it and he never takes a shot he can't make." That was really impressive to hear from a well-known coach that had been very successful at Southern Oregon University.

As the basketball season was once again approaching, SOU would travel to Klamath Falls, Oregon, for a preseason two-game tournament. They would face Puget Sound Christian College in the first game on Friday. I took the day off to drive down to the game since I had to get over the snowy mountains. It would take me longer than four hours to get there due to the snow. I asked my boss if I could take the day off and I left Salem early that day.

I wanted to get there early enough to watch them warm up and to get a good seat. When I arrived there I had to look for the college. It was off to the side of the main road behind a big hill. The geographical view was pretty dry with spots of snow that hadn't melted yet. It was a nice big coliseum with plenty of seating.

Puget Sound Christian College struggled against SOU. That team had problems containing Shea. When they doubled on him we had four players that could hit the three-point shot. SOU won their first game of the season big, 92 – 48.

Matt played his first NAIA Division II basketball game and he looked really good. When I saw that he was one of the starters I was blown away and I just had to be really proud. When I saw him play defense I said to myself, "Is that my son? Someone has been working with him on his defense, wow! The improvement is very impressive!"

He managed to score 10 points including three baskets beyond the arc. Shea led all scorers with 23 points. I really enjoyed watching the game and it was worth the drive to Klamath Falls.

After the game was over I went out to the lobby area to wait for the team to come out of the locker room. One of the first players out was Jeff Williams. As he was walking by me he scared me half to death, "Mr. Espinoza! Noza cut his foot in the locker room, he's bleeding like crazy! I don't know if he's going to be able to play tomorrow."

Everything was going great and once again I started worrying and felt terrible about the news Jeff had given me. I had to be patient and wait for Matt to come out of the dressing room. They had a trainer looking at the cut and taping it up. My heart once again almost stopped and I was anxious to talk to my son.

When he came out he was walking kind of slow and was looking at me in a way that he knew what I was about to ask him. I asked him, "Matt I heard that you cut your foot, how bad is it?" He said, "The cut is about an inch and a half long and it's pretty deep. I stepped over a bag coming out of the shower and I slipped on the wet floor and hit a piece of metal sticking out of the locker."

When I got back to Ashland where I was staying I waited for the team bus to arrive so I could give Matt a ride back to his apartment and take a look at his foot. I looked at it and it looked pretty bad. The cut was located next to the Achilles of his right foot. When I saw it I was concerned and said, "Matt you need to get stitches on that foot." Once again his reason for not going to the doctor was because he felt the doctor would not let him play the next day against rival OIT (Oregon Institute of Technology).

Well as you can see this game was the highest priority item for Matt at the time. No matter what I said he was going to play the next day. I purchased some butterfly tape with strong adhesive, peroxide and Neosporin. I patched him up good that night. He had a shoot around in the morning where the team was also scheduled for a scouting report on OIT.

I drove him to the gym early in the morning so the trainer could fix him up with tape, but there was no trainer there. Shea and Matt were the first ones there. Shea helped me by pushing both sides of the skin together on Matt's foot, where the cut was. I then proceeded to seal it up with butterfly tape. He was ready to go for the shoot-around.

Matt wanted to see how the foot felt, he was in pain but was still able to move and shoot baskets on it. I felt bad for him and once again told him that he should get that healed up before playing on it. He explained to me that he was going to try and play with the injury. If the pain was more than he could handle he would stop.

Later that evening at the tournament SOU would play rival OIT, the home team. Everyone was telling me, "You better get your ticket early for that game it's going to be sold out." So I bought my reserved ticket early. I showed up an hour before the game and had problems finding parking, it was jam packed with cars everywhere!

Southern Oregon and OIT were two of the top-ranked teams in the nation and they were playing against each other. For Matt to be playing in a game like this was beyond what a dad could dream about for his son.

Any basketball dad out there can probably relate to what I am saying. It was a successful moment that Matt earned through his hard work and determination. I am sure that he felt great playing in front of a sold out crowd. I thought to myself, "Finally, he is in a place that he has worked so hard for." I felt like this was one of his goals he had set very high for himself and reached convincingly.

The OIT Owls had fans that were vicious and took basketball very serious. They were very vocal and even yelled at the referees when they thought it was a bad call. They would say things like, "Come on ref! You need glasses!" or "Go back to ref school you are terrible!" I can't repeat the other comments they yelled, it would not be too appropriate.

The game started out very intense and Shea was double-teamed and sometimes triple-teamed. We were able to get three-point opportunities from time to time. Matt played on the injured foot. The trainer taped it up really good. He was playing with pain but the way he was shooting was helping the team. It didn't take OIT long to figure out he could hit the three-point shot. That opened things up for Jeff and Shea on the inside.

This game at the beginning of the season was exciting to watch and had several lead changes. The home crowd was so loud it was crazy! This was a game SOU could have won, but the ball just didn't bounce their way that night and OIT was a very tough team. SOU ended up losing, 67 – 72, but the game was closer than the score showed.

After the tournament they announced the All-Tournament Team. The selection for Southern Oregon was Shea Washington and Matt Espinoza. This was Matt's fourth time in his college career that he had made an All-Tournament Team. He just kept getting better. The interesting thing was that he played with a big cut on his foot.

I was looking at the schedule and noticed that two of the preseason games would be against Pac-10 teams. Southern Oregon was getting ready to play U of O (University of Oregon) and OSU (Oregon State University). These two colleges are Division I schools. This was exciting for all of us, Jake was attending U of O at the time, and Loni and I were only an hour away from there. The college was close enough that most of the people we knew could come watch Matt in action. Wow! Matt would be playing against Division I players. This would be a real test of how he could play at this level.

On November 9, 2005 we headed out to Eugene, Oregon, home of the Oregon Ducks. The game would take place at McArthur Court, which is located in the middle of the huge college campus. Matt arranged for us to get front row seats behind the SOU bench. We got there early but they didn't open the doors until one hour before tip off time. There was a big line outside the doors. I had such a great feeling all over, my son was playing basketball in the big times, and I can't even begin to describe the great feeling. He would be playing against Ernie Kent's team.

When the doors opened people started pouring in. The excitement of people talking about the game and students running to the door to get in quickly was such a rush. Basketball at McArthur Court is a different world. The student section and all the fans are all very supportive of their team. There was yellow and green everywhere we looked, they even had a duck mascot. I guess that's one of the reasons the Ducks have been so successful on their home court.

Once we found our seats inside, we were watching the players warm up and I looked over at Loni, "This is so amazing! I would have never guessed that someday Matt would be playing against the Oregon Ducks."

I noticed Matt in his number 30 Raider uniform, wearing red, white, and black colors. He was taking some warm-up shots from way downtown and making just about all of them. The Duck student section harassed him a bit, but Matt would just smile and continue shooting three-pointers. The place was sold out I looked around and did not see many seats empty, there were so many people it was unbelievable.

The National Anthem was sung and it was time to get the game started. I saw ten players walking to the center circle to get ready for the tip off. To start the game for SOU was 6'7" Shea Washington, 6'4" Matt Espinoza, 5'10" Steve Farley, 6'3" Matt Cowell and 6'8" Jeff Williams. To start the game for the Ducks was 6'0" Aaron Brooks, 6'9" Maarty Leunen, 6'6" Malik Hairston, 6'5" Bryce Taylor and 6'8" Ivan Johnson. When the game got going Malik

Hairston was guarding Matt and was playing some solid intense defense. Matt started playing some great basketball against Hairston. On the other end of the floor Matt was playing defense on Hairston. This Oregon athlete that Matt was battling with was a solid player and a handful. He didn't give Matt too many looks because of his intense defense, but Matt managed to get open a few times connecting two big three-pointers and one field goal for a final 8 points in the game.

When Matt hit his first three-pointer it gave him an enormous amount of confidence. This showed that he could play ball with Division I players. It was a very exciting moment for us. The game was such a fast pace game, I couldn't believe how quick Aaron Brooks was, it was amazing to see. All of the SOU players played well against the Ducks, we were all very proud of them.

The halftime score was Oregon 30 and SOU 29. It seemed like SOU was going to pull an upset. With seven minutes to play in the game Oregon was up 51 to 50 and Ernie Kent was sweating it a bit. Shea Washington was playing a great game but because of the size difference it was difficult to maintain the intensity. Jeff Williams was getting tired with big Ivan Johnson bumping him around all game. With three minutes left Oregon was starting to pull away and Coach Brian McDermott put in the bench to give them an opportunity to play at McArthur Court.

The final score was 75 to 58 in favor of the Oregon Ducks, but the game was a lot closer than the score indicated. It was a fun time and Shea Washington led all scorers with 18 points, Matt Espinoza had 8 points, Erion Moore II had 7 points, Jeff Williams had 6 points, Cowell had 5 points, RaShawn had 5 points, Steve Farley had 5 points and Brian Williams had 2 points. For Oregon Ivan Johnson led the way with 14 points, Aaron and Maarty both had 12 points, Bryce Taylor had 10 points and Malik Hairston had 9 points.

The following night the SOU Raiders played the OSU Beavers and again another exciting game against a PAC-10 team at Gill Coliseum. It looked as if SOU was going to win this one, but the Beavers came back late in the game to pull the victory 75 - 60. Shea led with 29 points, Espinoza scored 11 points and Matt Cowell added 5 points. The Beavers had a balanced scoring attack with their quick point guard Jason Fontenet he scored 16 points, Chris Stephens had 15 points and 6'10" Sasa Culc finished with 13 points.

It was a fun and exciting trip to both these games, we are so grateful that Matt had such a great opportunity to play against two NCAA Division I schools. Loni and I had great seats for us to watch both games. I don't think we will get seats like that again in the near future.

SOU headed back to Ashland to prepare for the big Flagship Inn Classic Tournament that was coming up. This two-day tournament was an annual event held at McNeal Pavilion, the home court of the Southern Oregon Raiders. An interesting game would take place in the tournament that Matt had been anticipating.

Let me first tell you a little bit about the SOU fans. Southern Oregon Raider fans were great, especially the student section. They go crazy during basketball games. I remember them holding up signs and some even painting themselves. Austin Loreman, is a true Raider fan; he painted his whole body red and black. He painted his back with white letters reading, "NOZA," it was amazing.

When the opponent starting five players were introduced, all the student section would read the newspaper. For me it was always a downer when we played games during holiday breaks because most of the students were not at school, and trust me, they were deeply missed.

Okay, now back to what Matt was anticipating. One of Matt's old high school teammates was coming to McNeal Pavilion, the 1400 seat coliseum, where the SOU Raiders played their home games. Josh Erickson, the starting point guard for the Willamette Bearcats, was waiting for this moment to play against one of his friends from high school. Willamette also had two other players that came from the Valley League Conference in Salem, Drew Miller and John Olinger, both great shooters and athletes that knew Matt well.

Josh had recovered from a torn ACL on one of his knees and was being played sparingly until he recovered fully. The last time Matt and Josh played in an official game together was when they were both wearing a royal blue uniform for the McNary Celtics.

Gordy James was the head coach for Willamette and he knew Matt very well. He was one of the coaches trying to recruit Matt to play for him. Matt worked for Gordy at a few basketball camps throughout the years. The plan for Gordy, I'm pretty sure, was to not let Matt get a look at the hoop from the three-point mark. It was going to be a long night for Matt.

From the beginning of the game I could hear the coach along with the Willamette bench, "Don't let him get the ball! Get up on him!" John Olinger started off guarding Matt. I remember John playing right up-the-line on Matt, John was a great defensive player as well as shooter and ball handler. When John turned his head to look at the point guard for one split second, Matt took off through the backdoor. John hustled back as best as he could, but it was too late and too much traffic to get through and catch him.

Another time during the first half, Matt was left open for two seconds and had enough time to put up a three-point shot and sink it off the back of the rim. Gordy jumped up and yelled at his team for letting Matt get a two-second look. He called a timeout, I'm not joking, and he chewed his players out! After that moment it was really tough for Matt to get a good look at the basket, but that was okay because he spread the floor and helped Jeff and Erion do their job on the inside.

Willamette was fortunate enough to play SOU when all-American Shea Washington had a severely sprained ankle. Shea sat out of this game to recover. With that said Willamette was playing a very good game against SOU and lead the game most of the time. The Raiders managed to come from behind and get the victory with a score of 68 to 59. It was a very exciting game to watch since there were five former Valley League players on the floor. Matt would get the first victory against his friend, Josh, but they would play again next year, something they definitely looked forward to.

The games after this one were big wins and Matt had played through his foot injury. It finally healed with time. At every game or practice he would get treatment and a taping job. The trainer had done a great job preventing his foot from getting infected.

SOU had won fifteen games in a row and when the polls were released the Raiders were ranked number one in the nation for NAIA Division II Men's College Basketball. Wow! That was something that made me feel honored to be a parent of a player on this team.

For the first part of the season Matt was the second leading scorer behind Shea Washington. Then the scouting reports were out that Matt could shoot the three-point shot. It was getting tougher for him to get open looks. He would have to start learning how to create shots for himself. With as many shooters as we had on the team that would not be too much of a problem simply because other players had better looks at times. And with a dominating player like Shea, Matt would get open looks again.

During the second half of the season we lost Jeff Williams to an ACL injury on his knee. He would be out for awhile with the chance that he might be able to play if SOU made it to the National Tournament in Point Lookout, Missouri. This would force Coach McDermott to move Matt to the forward position. On defense he would guard one of the biggest players along with Shea and on offense he would play up top mostly.

Toward the end of the season Southern Oregon lost some close games. Four of the games were overtime losses. Those are heartbreakers. In the final three games of the season, Southern Oregon lost by 1 point to Corban College when all-American Eric Fiegi hit a last second shot. Another lost came to Concordia University, they had a point guard that was red-hot that night. Southern Oregon's worst loss came against Albertson's College of Idaho, they played well and could not miss a basket, and SOU was ice cold on their shots. These three losses were costly for the national tournament seeding.

A string of bad luck hit the Raiders causing them to struggle a bit. Matt was averaging about 11 points a game and playing about 25 minutes a game. It just seemed to be a down swing for everyone. RaShawn McAllister seemed to be playing well and keeping us in games at times. Shea was pretty consistent, but started missing free-throws which was very rare for him.

Cowell and Farley played consistently and were two of our best ball handlers, but their shooting started faltering a bit. They were playing a lot of minutes throughout the season and normally they were good three-point shooters. Thomas Ward was a great point guard that was a spark coming off the bench for SOU. When Steve was struggling a bit, Thomas would help us with his consistent play. We were very fortunate that our guards were not injured seriously during the season. I think that kept us alive for a national tournament bid.

At this point in time I was married to Loni and she traveled to all the games with me. The way I proposed to her was probably not the most romantic way, but I guess with both of us enjoying basketball so much it made sense. We were shooting baskets in my backyard and I remember being disappointed because See's Candies was closed and I couldn't do what I had planned. I had planned on putting the ring inside one of the chocolate slots in the box and giving it to her so she would be surprised. Instead I just asked her while we were shooting baskets in the backyard one evening.

I showed her the ring and asked, "Loni, I love you, and I enjoy being around you so much, will you marry me?" She responded with a smile, "If you make your next free-throw." I learned quickly that Loni never has a straight yes or no answer. She always has a story or an explanation before the fact. I was really under pressure. I took the shot and swoosh! It was nothing but net. Then she explained to me, "Okay, now if I make my free-throw I will say yes." Well I guess we were meant to be because she made hers too.

I still remember the night before our wedding because SOU had just lost in overtime to Warner Pacific University in Portland. Jake and I brought Matt back with us after that game to get ready for the wedding the next day. I remember some of the players in the bus yelling out, "Hey Noza! Where are you going?" He answered, "My Dad is getting married tomorrow. I have a wedding to go to!" Matt even played the guitar and sang at our wedding. It was a very nice and small wedding with just family and a few friends there.

Steve Farley's parents, like us, were very supportive of the team. We saw them at all the home and away games. They are nice people and it was always a pleasure seeing them at games. Southern Oregon had bingo games for prizes at all the home games during halftime. Mr. and Mrs. Farley, and Mr. and Mrs. Espinoza would compete at bingo. I think we ended up winning three times and they ended up winning two times during the season.

When the season ended, the long wait started. We were all waiting to see if SOU would get a bid for the 2006 NAIA Division II Men's Basketball National Championship Tournament March 8-14. Southern Oregon started out being ranked number one in the nation, but by the end of the season they had dropped to number ten. The only hope now was to get an automatic bid because of their record and ranking.

The results came through and we were headed to Point Lookout, Missouri! The news was really exciting! We were flying to Missouri to watch Matt play in a college national basketball tournament. We were optimistic but at the same time knew that we had injuries on the team and we were not 100 percent. With Shea nursing a sprained ankle and Jeff Williams with a torn ACL on his knee, we were still going to give it our best shot when we got there.

The opportunity to go to nationals was very rare and to get that opportunity was what every team in the nation would wish for. Coach McDermott went to work with his team. He needed to get his Raiders ready to play at the National Tournament. SOU had earned a spot but they would have to face a home state number 14 seed, WJU (William Jewell University) of Missouri. That was going to be a tough game, but hey, it was March Madness! I love that time of the year!

William Jewell had two all-American players 6'4" Drew Matthews, and 6'6" Brandon Argo. SOU had one all-American player, Shea Washington. With Jeff Williams out and possibly a chance to play, the coach would start Shea, Matt Espinoza, Matt Cowell, Steve and RaShawn. Wow! My son was one of the starting five at a national college basketball tournament. He had come a long way since the McNary High School days.

With Jeff hurt Matt would have to play the post position and was assigned to defend Drew Matthews. In my opinion Coach McDermott's strategy was probably the best for the team. Matt would guard the all-American Matthews. Matt had the upper body to physically contain Matthews. Shea would guard Robinson a 6'4" 280 pound post. When Robinson was out, Shea would guard Brandon Argo their tallest player.

When the game started SOU could not hit a basket, everything seemed to be bouncing out of the rim. WJU started out hitting all their shots. Matthews would connect on some turn-around shots with Matt's defense right on him. WJU took a commanding lead 9 - 2 in the first five minutes of the game. Southern Oregon seemed to be playing against a home crowd. Matt had the ball in his hands and hit Cowell on the back door for the assist! Matt was playing a heck of a game but his three-point shots were in and out.

No one on the team could hit anything. SOU found themselves in a hole, 13 - 2. The next stretch down Matt hit Shea Washington for a lay-in for two points. The score was now 13 - 4. WJU missed their shot and SOU got the rebound and began to get a run going. Erion hit a basket for two points! Then Cowell made a basket for another two and Shea continued the sequence the next time down. The score was now 15 - 10.

SOU would eventually take the lead 31 - 27, but this would be the largest lead that Southern Oregon would have. In the second half Matt hit a big three-point basket! In my opinion, Matt was working so hard on defense guarding Matthews that earlier in the game his three-point shot was not going in. Matt fouled out and Shea Washington fouled out on calls that were very questionable. I looked at the game tape several times and saw the bad calls made by the officials. That is just the way it goes when playing a home state team.

When Matt got his fifth foul he was very upset and could not believe that they would not call an offensive foul. Matthews dribbled the ball toward Matt and bumped him. Matt had excellent position and his hands were up! When Shea fouled out the officials made a call on him when he was not even close to the player that drove to the basket! Again I looked at the tape over and over and did not see a foul.

That is just the way the night went, SOU did not get many breaks. When you play a home state team you just can't get in the hole at the beginning of the game. SOU picked the wrong game to get into a cold shooting streak at the beginning. Not taking any credit away from WJU, they played a heck of a game and things seem to bounce their way.

Jeff Williams played with a tear on his ACL which didn't help. He was not 100 percent but gave everything he could. He injured the knee again and fell to the floor in pain, shortly after that he came out of the game. Matt, Shea and Jeff were out of the game with eight minutes left and some of the other SOU players were in foul trouble as well. SOU still managed to come back and tie the game on a Farley three-point shot. But the game was not meant to be in favor of Southern Oregon University. They ended up losing in overtime 64 - 67 to William Jewell University. Matt had scored seven points in the first round of play.

I think if some of our key players would have not fouled out, we could have possibly gotten the victory. The boys played their hearts out and put in a great effort but fell short. Matt fouled out early in the second half just when he started connecting on his shot. He was very disappointed that he could not help his team more. Some games go that way and unfortunately this was the National Championships and it was so hard to accept the fact that they would not advance to the next round.

Southern Oregon made it there and to me that was a huge accomplishment for the team. In my mind, whether they won or lost did not matter, well, maybe it did matter a little. But honestly, watching the great effort they put in, and experiencing a great winning season of 23 wins and 9 losses with this team, I'll never forget. I was very proud of Matt and his teammates. They showed great character and great control when calls were made that seemed inconsistent. That shows a sign of a well coached team and mature players that demonstrated great sportsmanship.

TWENTY

TWO 3-POINT SHOT RECORDS
2006-2007

DESPITE AN INJURED BACK

This year Matt would meet a young lady that played on the SOU girl's basketball team. He never really talked that much about dating girls, but I would eventually find out. Loni and I drove down to Ashland to meet Matt for dinner one weekend. When we called to pick him up, he said, "Dad, Andi is coming to dinner with us." Andrea (Andi) was the first girl that I knew of him actually going out on a real date with. I knew of Matt having friends that were female in college, but not more than that, at least he never spoke of it. Andi is such a nice girl and seems to fit in really well with Matt and things he likes to do. We often had dinner with them when we made the Ashland trip for games. It was nice to know that Matt would have a girlfriend to spend time with during the school year, we were really happy for the both of them.

It was the beginning of Matt's senior year at Southern Oregon University and his final year of college basketball. Wow! Where had the years gone? My youngest child was going to graduate from college after this year. Matt would share an apartment with two returning players from the team, Josh McDermott and Matt Cowell. This would work out well since all three of them played on the team and their schedules were similar.

Without Shea Washington, SOU would not be as strong underneath the basket, but they still had talent and could compete against the best in the Cascade Conference. Southern Oregon was not ranked in the nation this season, they were ranked 6th in the preseason polls for the Cascade Conference. Brian McDermott had recruited, Chuckie Ivey, a point guard that transferred from Coppin State University, and also Jason Nunnemaker, a 6'8" post from Grants Pass High School in Oregon. These two players would play significant roles and showed promise for the future, but they were young and lacked experience.

Early in the season Espinoza was playing great basketball, and it looked like SOU was going to have a great season. Matt took a senior leadership role and was one of the captains of the basketball team. Early in the season he would help SOU win several games. Against Simpson University Matt would score 18 points and collect 7 rebounds helping SOU defeat the opponent, 73 - 58. Against Dominican University Matt scored 16 points just in the first half alone, he was 6 for 6 inside the paint and 4 for 4 from the penalty stripe. He ended up with 20 points at the end of the game including 5 for 6 beyond the arc. Southern Oregon won big with the score of 73 - 58.

Against Corban College Espinoza scored 19 points and pulled down 6 rebounds. They had outdone Corban, 84 - 68. Against Concordia University Matt scored 15 points to lead all scorers defeating Concordia, 69 - 65.

The game against Willamette University was coming up. This would be a non- conference game and a game Matt would look forward to playing. The game would take place back in his home town, Salem, Oregon. Espinoza's old high school teammate, Josh Erickson, played for Willamette. Josh played the point guard position and he was doing very well for his team. SOU had beaten Willamette the previous year and I am sure that Josh wanted to get even with Matt for that loss. Coach Gordy James had spoken in the locker room and one of the plans was to not let Matt get the ball. Gordy did not want Matt to get any kind of a look at the 3-point shot.

Who could have predicted this unfortunate disappointment? We first heard that Josh had torn an ACL for the third time and his career came to an end. Wow, that was very sad news to us. I can't imagine how his parents felt. His life revolved around basketball just like Matt and Jake, my two kids. I said a prayer for Josh and his family.

Only people like us could begin to understand how devastating an injury like that could be to a player and his family. He was a player that played for years to get to where he was now. Josh is 5'11" and he was a quick point guard with excellent passing skills, a great 3-point shot and consistent defense. He was a great leader on the court and a good friend of Matt.

A week before the Willamette game something else happened. Matt was dealing with back problems and then his left leg came down with a life threatening infection called MRSA. He couldn't even walk without being in a lot of pain. He was taking antibiotics to fight the infection. There was no way on earth he was going to play on that leg. But I always had a difficult time convincing him. He always had to try first before deciding. He just wanted to play so bad; he loved the game of basketball.

When he tried warming up with his leg taped it was very difficult to run on it. He would experience plenty of pain. In addition the antibiotics were making him dizzy and he was losing his balance. Matt informed the coach that he was not physically able to play. SOU ended up losing to Willamette, and Matt and Josh ended up sitting on the bench watching the game. They got the opportunity to visit with each other and catch up on things, but did not play against each other.

Next on the schedule was WOU (Western Oregon University). Ryan Schmidt, a 6'7" guard, was now playing for WOU. Ryan had graduated from McNary High School a year ahead of Matt. He played at Linn-Benton with Matt's brother Jake. Matt had recovered from MRSA and was well enough to score 11 points to help the Raiders win against WOU, 84 to 69. It was fun watching Ryan and Matt play against each other.

The first conference lost came against Evergreen State College, 79 – 66. This was about the time where Matt started having more problems with his lower back. He could never get enough rest to recover. He was not playing 100 percent and I think that hurt Southern Oregon a bit. SOU started losing some games. They did win a few, but Matt was needed. His leadership and his 3-point shot was a key piece of the team. Like one broadcaster said, "The 3-point shot is one of the reasons Brian McDermott recruited Espinoza."

Because of injuries, SOU would struggle during the regular season. They would lose several games including one to rival OIT. But they played through the injuries receiving treatment from the trainer before and after games. Matt would arrive there early and hit the trainer's room for treatment on his back. He would then play in the game, score some three-point shots, and help the team however he could. After the games he would get an ice bath for 20 minutes. This went on for the rest of the season.

At the end of the season Southern Oregon made the playoffs and would face Warner Pacific University in the first round of the playoffs. They would have to win the rest of the games in the playoffs to make it to the national tournament again. The game was held in Portland, Oregon, at Warner Pacific's home court. They were a team that was ranked as one of the top teams in the nation. This game was very important, if SOU lost this would be Matt's final game of his college career.

The game started out great for SOU, senior post Erion Moore II pulled down seven rebounds helping the Raiders dominate on the boards in the first half. Matt tallied eight points, Trenton Frazier also connected with eight points, Matt Cowell helped balance the scoring attack with five points and Matt Pizzola scored seven points. Southern Oregon would lead at the half, 37 – 33. The Raiders were doing great on offense, shooting 37 percent from 3-point range and 54 percent from the charity stripe in the first 20 minutes of play.

The WPU Knights shot 48 percent in the first half, but had problems with their 3-pointers. The Knights were shooting the ball solid from the charity stripe all season long but this game they struggled shooting 5 for 10. Jalonta Martin led the Knights in the first half with 10 points and 7 rebounds, Josh Jackson added 9 points and Scott O'Gallagher scored 8 points. The Raiders played excellent defense and only allowed the Knight's bench 4 points.

The Raiders would come out in the second half and increase their lead, 44 – 33, with Espinoza connecting on some big time range 3-pointers. With 18 minutes left Warner Pacific calls a time out to figure out what to do to stop the 3-point shot. They came out putting pressure on Matt, Frazier, Cowell and Krasowski. 6' 8" Jason Nunnemaker was not playing for SOU due to an illness, so as you can see, the team was lacking on rebounding power and defending the big guys.

The Knights came back and tied the game with 8 minutes left in the game. It was a seesaw game and an exciting one to watch. All of the SOU fans were hoping for an upset, it seemed like it could possibly happen. But with O'Gallagher driving to the basket and getting the call consistently helped Warner Pacific take an 84 – 82 lead with 12 seconds left in the game. The final score ended up being 87 – 82, and Warner Pacific escaped an upset.

Matt would score 16 points in his final college game to end his college basketball career. He shot 5 for 7 overall, 4 for 5 from 3-point land, and 2 for 3 from the charity stripe. Nursing an aching back with treatment before and after the game, I would say that he gave all he could to help the team as much as he could.

It was a heartbreaker and I know that my son was disappointed. But I wasn't disappointed when I saw how hard he and his teammates worked on the floor. I was so proud of him and his team for the strong effort. Even though they lost, to me, they were winners. It's always tough playing a top-ranked team on their home court.

If SOU had not encountered the serious injuries and illnesses to several of the key players, I have no doubt that they would have been contenders for a chance at nationals. Sometimes things happen for a reason and it just wasn't meant to be. It wasn't the Lord's will that SOU go to nationals again, but maybe for another team to have that opportunity.

Matt Espinoza went out a winner and had two successful years at Southern Oregon University. On his last basketball season at SOU he averaged 10.17 points per game and scored 234 points. He broke two records in the 3-point shooting category. Matt broke the SOU 3-point percentage record, shooting 50.5 percent from 3-point land. This record was previously held by Jerome Wright in 1986 at 46.2 percent. Espinoza also shattered the 3-point percentage record in a single game. Against Dominican University, Matt hit 5 for 6 treys for an SOU single game record of 83 percent. This record was previously held by Jason Knudson in 1983 at 80 percent.

Not only did he set two records at Southern Oregon University, but Espinoza earned an honor for Men's NAIA Division I and II Basketball. Matt was named to the 2006-2007 Daktronics-NAIA All-American Scholar Athlete of The Year Award. The reason he was selected was for having a successful senior season of basketball and earning a GPA of 4.0 the last term and a cumulative GPA of 3.67. Matt received his Bachelor of Arts in Communications/ Journalism and is now a college graduate.

(TOP) Matt's dad helps him with his first grade jump shot.

(LEFT) Matt was two years old when he started shooting the basketball.

(TOP) Matt and brother Jake (far left) with friends in the backyard.

(BOTTOM) Jake tries to block Matt's shot.

(TOP) Jake and Matt hold up two Blazer tickets each after winning the Boys and Girls Club Holiday Two-on-Two Tournament.

(RIGHT) Picture with Reggie Miller of the Indiana Pacers at Matt's first Blazer's game.

(TOP) Matt with his brother and cousins at Diamond Lake Resort in Oregon.

(BOTTOM) Inside the Memorial Coliseum before a Blazer game.

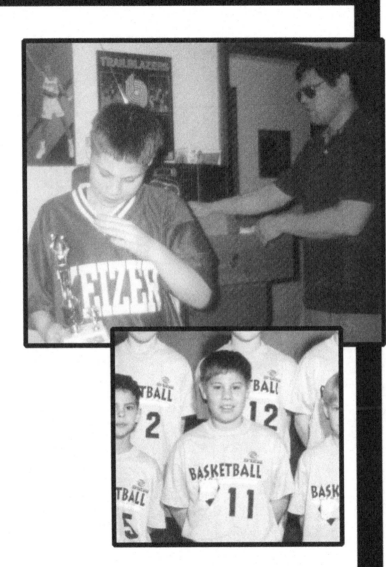

(TOP) Matt holds up his all-tournament team trophy.

(BOTTOM) Matt played ball at the Boys and Girls Club growing up in Salem, OR.

The Espinoza Family 1993

(TOP) Matt gets ready to play D with teammate Jared.

(RIGHT) Noza takes a jump shot in a JV game.

(LEFT) Matt scores one of his 11 three-pointers against the Texas Wolverines at the Adidas Big Time Tournament in Las Vegas.

Matt says, "Get that stuff out of here Dad."

(TOP) McNary tips off against Southridge for the fourth place trophy at the the Oregon State High School Basketball Championships.

(RIGHT) Noza at the free-throw line during a league basketball game.

Father and son at the awards banquet.

McNary's 2003 senior class set several records for McNary's basketball program and finished 4th at the State Tournament.

(TOP) David with his two sons after their battle at South-western Oregon Community College.

(BOTTOM) Matt passes to a teammate as his brother Jake defends.

(TOP) Noza signs a Letter of Intent to play basketball at Southern Oregon University.

(BOTTOM) 2005-2006 Southern Oregon Raiders. NAIA D2 National Qualifiers.

Southern Oregon vs. Oregon State

(TOP) Espinoza looks to pass against Willamette University.

(BOTTOM) Austin Loreman, a true Raider fan, gets ready for a home game.

(LEFT) Matt hits a big basket at home against league rival OIT.

(TOP) Matt graduated from Southern Oregon University with a bachelor's degree in Communications/Journalism.

(BOTTOM) Matt as the best man at his brother's wedding.

TWENTY-ONE

CONCLUSION AND NOTES

WORDS OF BASKETBALL WISDOM

In the beginning Matt struggled with his body not developing quite as fast as other kids. But his faith, determination and hard work superseded what might have caused others to give up. To this day, I have seen few people that can hit the 3-point shot like Matt does, and I've been around the game a very long time.

Two weeks after his college basketball career was over, Espinoza had signed up for an open tryout with the Portland Trailblazers. In addition he was talking to the IBL (International Basketball League) which consists of professional minor league basketball teams. He was talking to a team in Seattle, Washington, and one in Salem, Oregon. Matt also was talking overseas to someone in China's professional basketball league.

Matt is recovering from a back injury he sustained during his senior year in college. He is at 75 percent and continues to rehabilitate his back. He is weighing his options right now. If his back recovers fully he plans to pursue playing professional basketball. If that doesn't work out, he plans to obtain his masters degree and acquire a career in the education field, which would include coaching basketball, his love.

A lot of kids today have dreams of playing college basketball and even NBA basketball, but only a few of them make it there. I started teaching my son, Matt, the fundamentals of basketball at a very young age. Lets face it, if you don't start young you will be a step behind the next person. Somewhere out there is a player that's working harder than you. High school varsity teams usually carry 12 or 13 players on their roster and only seven or eight get to play. That means most of the kids that you played with in grade school, junior high, the freshman team, and the JV team will not be part of the varsity high school team.

If a basketball player has the love for the game he or she will sacrifice and put in some hard work to put him or herself in a position to play high school varsity basketball and even perhaps college basketball.

I also want to strongly emphasize something just as important as having the love for the game of basketball. While Matt worked hard at improving his skills on the basketball court, he also exercised his brain. His mother and I had preached to him about how important the grades were. I used to tell him and his brother that without exceptional grades you cannot play college basketball. You can be the player of the year in high school, and the leading scorer in the state, but that won't mean anything when you get to college if you can't make the grades. Colleges expect athletes to maintain a passing grade point average, failure to do so could cause the athlete to become ineligible and possibly lose their scholarship.

Matt developed good study habits. He always completed his homework and he turned it in on time. I was fortunate, in that I rarely helped him with his homework. He just took it upon himself to study and learn as much as he could. I remember him staying up late doing homework because of his basketball practices and bible studies. While Matt was playing college basketball, he would tell me that he studied on the bus and at the hotels. He knew that good grades played an important role in reaching the challenging goals he set for himself. Matt also knew that there would be life after his basketball days.

I had dreams when I was playing sports. My dreams are not my kid's dreams. Matt and his brother taught me an important lesson. A lesson that I learned by listening to them and by watching them. I learned that I had to support them in following their own dreams and not mine. I just want Matt and Jake to smile while they chase their dreams. I figure as long as they are having fun and smiling, I can feel really good about myself.

Thank the good Lord that Noza made it through four years of college basketball with minimal injuries. He has left his mark at Southwestern Oregon Community College and at Southern Oregon University, as one of the best three-point sharp shooters in school history. That to me is a result of plain good old hard work. I am very proud of my son and I know that whatever he decides to pursue in life, he will be very successful.

EPILOGUE

Written by Matt Espinoza

The biggest fit I ever threw was when I was five years old. I remember my brother playing in his first Boys and Girls Club basketball game. I was forced to sit and watch from the side. Even though I was two years younger, I could always tag along and play with him. But there he was; uniforms, referees, scoreboard. All I could do was look on. There was nothing I could do about it.

As I grew older, looking on became more difficult. Yeah, I was on the team, I had a jersey. I practiced everyday and enjoyed every minute of it. But I hated the feeling of sitting on the side watching the game, knowing I wouldn't be playing tonight. It was the same feeling I had when I was five, watching my brother. But this time, there was something I could do. And I did it. I did everything I could to get better.

I know it's just a game. I know that when I die and I'm standing in front of God, He's not going to look up my average before He decides whether or not to let me in. But for some reason, He made basketball a passion for me.

And He's never going to let me quit.

ABOUT THE AUTHOR

David Espinoza was raised in Dimmitt, Texas. In 1976 when he was a sophomore in high school his family packed up and moved to Oregon. He finished his last two years of high school attending Woodburn High School part of the time and graduating from Gervais High School. During high school he was a three sport athlete. David remembers being in a football locker room after the last game of the season. He said to one of his friends, "My favorite sport is basketball I'm so glad football is over." One of the football coaches heard him and chewed him out royally.

He attended Chemeketa Community College in Salem, Oregon, and graduated with an Associates Degree in Computer Science. While working in the computer field he also played minor league Pro-Football, studied acting for three years, performed in some local theatre plays and even shot a commercial or two. He still lives in Oregon, the wonderful state filled with rivers and mountains. He discovered that he enjoys writing about true stories and adventures he has experienced throughout his life.

Raising his family in Oregon has been such a delightful experience for him, but plenty of hard work. His first child was born in 1982, and his second child in 1984. Despite the fact that he lost his wife, Candi, to brain cancer in 1994, if he had to do to it all over again, he would do it again in a second. The blessings he received surpassed his expectations. David's aspirations for his two boys were to help them get a college education and to help them become successful athletes. His older son Jake seemed to be on track. Jake was blessed with athletic talent and he had the height all through grade school, middle school, high school and college. He was always a starter and one of the best players on any basketball team he played for.

David's younger son, Matt, is what inspired him to write this book. When Matt was a young kid he was not tall like Jake, nor did he have the abilities that Jake did. David was there for practices, games and tournaments. He witnessed something that really amazed him. David wants to share Matt's story with the world in hopes that some basketball player out there finds encouragement and never gives up on following his or her dream.

CREDITS

Quotes by Dave Immel, Jim Litchfield, Josh Erickson, and Matt Espinoza, in Chapter Fourteen, credited to the Statesman Journal Newspaper in Salem, Oregon.

Quotes by Brian McDermott, in Chapter Nineteen, credited to sousports.com in Ashland, Oregon.

Special thanks to Jacob Espinoza for the cover design, and the layout work on the inside photos.

Special thanks to Ken Royce Photography for the front cover photo, and the Southern Oregon men's basketball photos.

Special thanks to members of the Espinoza family for the family photos, except for the wedding photo. Thanks to Brianne Wills for the wedding photo.

Special thanks to Craig Huston Photography for the Boys and Girls Club photos.

Special thanks to Northwest Sports Photography in Beaverton, Oregon, for the Keizer and McNary basketball photos.

CPSIA information can be obtained
at www.ICGtesting.com
Printed in the USA
FSOW03n1448020615
7525FS